# THE CIVILIZATION OF THE
# AMERICAN INDIAN SERIES

# CHEROKEE DANCE AND DRAMA

Frank G. Speck

Will West Long

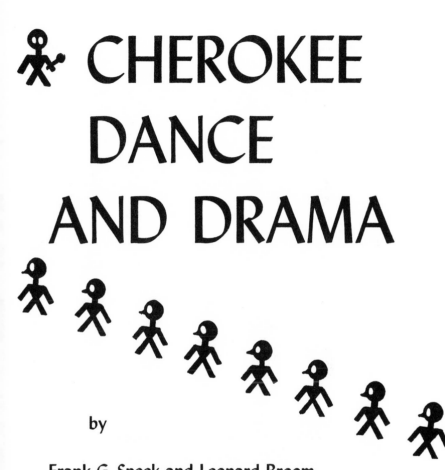

# CHEROKEE
# DANCE
# AND DRAMA

by

Frank G. Speck and Leonard Broom
in Collaboration with Will West Long

University of Oklahoma Press
Norman

OTHER BOOKS BY FRANK G. SPECK

*Beothuk and Micmac* (New York, 1922)
*Naskapi: The Savage Hunters of the Labrador Peninsula* (Norman, 1935, 1977)
*Oklahoma Delaware Ceremonies, Dances, and Feasts* (Philadelphia, 1937)
*Penobscot Man: The Life History of a Forest Tribe in Maine* (Philadelphia, 1940)
*Midwinter Rites of the Cayuga Long House* (Philadelphia, 1949)

OTHER BOOKS BY LEONARD BROOM

*The Managed Casualty: The Japanese-American Family in World War II* (Berkeley, 1956, 1973)
*Transformation of the Negro American* (New York, 1965, 1967)
*Opportunity and Attainment in Australia* (Stanford, 1976)
*The Inheritance of Inequality* (London and Boston, 1980)

**Library of Congress Cataloging in Publication Data**

Speck, Frank Gouldsmith, 1881–1950.
  Cherokee dance and drama.
ISBN: 0-8061-2580-2 (alk. paper)
(The Civilization of the American Indian series)
  Bibliography: p. 105
  Includes index.
  1. Cherokee Indians—Dances.  2. Indians of North America—North Carolina—Dances.  I. Broom, Lenoard.  II. West Long, Will.  III. Title.  IV. Series.
E99.C5S66    1983        793.3'1'08997        83-47839

5  6  7  8  9  10  11

# CONTENTS

# Contents

# PLATES

(ix)

# Plates

# FIGURES

(xi)

# SYMBOLS USED TO REPRESENT CHEROKEE SOUNDS

In recording Eastern Cherokee (Qualla dialect) words we have, for the sake of uniformity, adhered to the pronunciation of West Long, a Cherokee purist. The system of representation is based on Mooney and Olbrechts (1932: 11-13), although we have simplified his highly elaborated scheme of notation. For further discussion of Cherokee phonetics, see Bender and Harris (1946).

## VOWELS

| | | | |
|---|---|---|---|
| a | as in "father" | u | as *oo* in "moon" |
| ɑ | as in "sun" | i | as in "pin" |
| ɔ | as *aw* in "law" | i̜ | as *ea* in "seat" |
| ɛ | as *ai* in "air" | ə | obscure *e* as in "the" when occurring before initial consonant |
| e | as *a* in "take" | | |
| o | approximately as in "note" | | |

Nasalization is indicated by a tilde over the vowel.

Aspiration, an audible breath, following vowels and consonants is shown by the left single quote.

The colon after a vowel denotes lengthening; the letter is doubled for consonants.

The dot on the line after a symbol denotes a slight pause.

## SEMICONSONANTS

y, w  approximately as in English

## CONSONANTS

| | | | |
|---|---|---|---|
| d | voiced, as in "do" (often intermediate with *t*) | g | voiced, as in "go" (often intermediate with *k*) |
| D | intermediate between *d* and *t* | ɢ | intermediate between *g* and *k* |
| t | unvoiced, as *t* in "hit." If *t* is audibly aspirated it is written *t*' | k | unvoiced, as in "king." If *k* is audibly aspirated it is written *k*' |

# Symbols

| | | | |
|---|---|---|---|
| n, m | as in English | c | equal to *sh* as in "fish" |
| s, z | as in English | dz | voiced, as in "adze" |
| l | as in English | ts | unvoiced, as in "ants" |
| ł | unvoiced (no equivalent in English) | dj | voiced, as *j* in "Jim" |
| | | tc | unvoiced, as *ch* in "church" |

' after a symbol denotes a glottal stop, unrepresented in English but corresponding to *tt* in the broad Scottish pronunciation of "bottle," "button"

## ACCENTS

´ denotes primary stress, usually with rising pitch

` denotes secondary stress, usually with falling pitch

# FOREWORD TO THE NEW EDITION

This edition is a memorial to my collaborators, Frank G. Speck and Will West Long. I am glad for the opportunity to record my appreciation of their friendship and my debt for the guidance they gave me when I was a young and inexperienced field-worker. I am grateful to the University of California Press for releasing the copyright and to W. L. Parker for preparing the index for this edition.

With the kind agreement of the Speck estate, the copyright and all authors' royalties will be turned over to the officers of the Eastern Cherokee peoples. They are asked to use the funds in memory of Speck and West Long to aid the education of Cherokee students and especially to encourage mastery of the Cherokee language and the Sequoya syllabary.

Whatever limitations the syllabary may have (Kilpatrick and Kilpatrick, 1966:8-9, 86), it is a product of genius and deserves to persist as a living instrument. The Cherokee language itself will survive longer if the syllabary is known and used by Cherokee speakers. Literate Cherokee will be likely to identify and save valuable old documents written in the syllabary, and that in turn will help preserve their heritage. The cross-cultural experiment with a syllabary primer is an interesting attempt to apply Sequoya's creation to contemporary concerns (Walker, 1965).

# Foreword

Frank Gouldsmith Speck

Frank G. Speck was born in Brooklyn, New York, on November 8, 1881, and died in Philadelphia on February 6, 1950.[1] His place in American ethnology is secure. Both the range of his contribution and his personal style are captured in the following passages:

[Frank G. Speck] . . . was beloved by his students and colleagues, and was acclaimed by Algonquians, Siouans, and Iroquoians alike, from Labrador to Louisiana, as one of their own. In his heyday Speck used to treat his students by taking them on forays into the Delaware and Virginia swamps and to the Great Smokies of North Carolina where they combined field collecting in natural history with recovering the ancient hunting and fishing lore, ethnobotany, and bird lore among the Nanticoke, Rappahannock, Chickahominy, and Cherokee, not to mention the Delaware, Abenaki, and Cayuga in the north (Fenton, 1957:6).

Speck's name is almost synonymous with the ethnology of the Algonquian peoples of Eastern North America and of their Iroquoian neighbors, particularly the Cayuga, and the Cherokee in the highlands of Carolina (Butterfield et al., 1957:5).

He had the full repertoire of research skills: He was a naturalist, an expert and practical linguist, a folklorist, an ethnohistorian and an ethnogeographer. He was a penetrating observer and faithful reporter of ceremonial behavior and texts. He was knowledgeable in the total process of Amerindian technology from raw materials to final product and the uses that the products served, both functional and symbolic. His interests in religious behavior and his investigations of Cherokee ceremony, partially presented in this book, led him in his late years to the study of Iroquois ceremonialism.

Just as Speck embodied the talents of a field researcher, his personality suited him for the close association and sustained interaction that the best ethnological fieldwork requires. He was committed to

[1] This comment draws on the obituary by Hallowell (1951) and the bibliography appended to it (Witthoft, 1951). Hallowell (1951) and some other items have been added to the Bibliography in this edition.

(xvi)

# Foreword

the peoples with whom he worked as well as to the knowledge they could convey. He engaged them, was concerned with their concerns, and helped them in practical ways. As I had occasion to say in the first printing of this book: "There have been few American anthropologists so patient and thorough in the field. To my knowledge none could win more completely the respect, friendship, and cooperation of the people with whom they worked." But I should add that his interpersonal relations did not diminish the rigor and objectivity of his observations.

## WILL WEST LONG

The Big Cove community into which Will West Long[2] was born about 1870 was a culturally conservative enclave of the Qualla Reservation, the settlement to which a Cherokee remnant escaped the 1838-1839 Removal to Oklahoma. The trauma of that Removal dominated the lives of West Long's generation as well as that of his parents.

After the Removal, Qualla was a refuge, but it was no hiding place from whites who extended the long history of depredations. Most of the whites were themselves living close to the margin of subsistence, and from time to time they committed acts of aggression against Indians. It is no secret that violence is a constant theme during the centuries of failed government in the relations between Indians and whites. Living memory of the Removal and contemporary clashes with whites destroyed tranquillity for West Long's generation. They approached whites with anxiety, doubt, and resentment, but even in the mountain fastness they could not be entirely free from the threats and temptations of white society.

West Long's mother, Sally Terrapin, and her brother were major figures in his early socialization, especially because the matrilineal clan is the basic unit of Cherokee social organization. West Long's

[2] This account draws upon Witthoft (1948).

# Foreword

father, John Long, was a Cherokee Baptist preacher. In his teens West Long was sent to a school near High Point, North Carolina, more than two hundred miles from Qualla—his first extended stay outside the Qualla Boundary and his first unshielded exposure to white society. Understandably he became homesick and ran away home; but he was sent back to school, where he gained a basic literacy in English. In all, he spent over a year at school.

Soon after West Long returned to Qualla, James Mooney, the salient figure in Cherokee ethnography and historiography, arrived to begin his important research. Mooney recognized the unusual capacity of the young West Long and hired him as scribe, aide, and interpreter, but he was far more than an employer. He was West Long's mentor and friend. West Long learned the complex skills of communication across languages, and he was socialized in scholarly attitudes towards his own culture and an inquiring appreciation of it. He sharpened his literacy in the syllabary by useful practice. The lasting relationship between the two men encouraged West Long to pursue the study of Cherokee learning for its own sake and as a source of modest earnings. Thus his association with Mooney set a style of interaction that benefited later scholars for whom West Long served as informant, not in the narrow sense but as a guide and scholarly collaborator.

A few years later Mooney's friendly interest was probably instrumental in West Long's entering Hampton Institute and his subsequent sojourn in New England. In all, he was away from Qualla from about his twenty-fifth to his thirty-fourth year while attending school and working. He returned shortly before his mother died in 1904, married a few years later, and spent almost all of the remainder of his long life at Qualla.

Once again he took up his association with Mooney and deepened his study of Cherokee ways. Traditionally, sacred Cherokee lore was bought and sold between qualified practitioners, and almost from its invention they used the Sequoya syllabary to write down their medici-

# Foreword

nal and religio-magic formulas. Therefore, scattered through the dwellings of medicine men were cultural documents of value to practitioners and ethnographers alike: some were substantial records, such as the Swimmer manuscript, others only scraps of knowledge.

Over the years much of this material was lost, but West Long acquired manuscripts and notebooks from other learned Cherokee or their descendants. His acquisitiveness resulted from more than a pecuniary impulse or scholarly intent, although both of those motivations were involved. He also sought to extend his command of a resource that he believed held significant potential. Witthoft succinctly summarizes the complexities of West Long's attitudes in the following passage:

His attitude toward the tradition and ritual he revealed to ethnologists was clear, but caused him considerable difficulty. He believed the knowledge he carried was of very real power, and its potentiality for good or evil strong. On the one hand, he wanted to see it preserved and interpreted, and he needed the wages he received for his work; on the other, he was always afraid of exposing himself and his people to ridicule, and he was never sure that the people who hired him did not use his information for commercial, and perhaps even antisocial, purposes. He saw the men for whom he worked prosper, while he remained impoverished, and he sometimes had fantastic ideas of the wealth of his scholarly friends. Nevertheless, his relationships with ethnologists were apparently little influenced by such considerations (Witthoft, 1948: 359).

If Mooney's association with West Long was a model collegial and personal relationship, Olbrechts's was, to say the least, more complicated. During 1926 and 1927, with West Long as his interpreter and primary informant, Olbrechts carried on the fieldwork that culminated in the valuable publication, *The Swimmer Manuscript* (Mooney and Olbrechts, 1932). He acknowledged West Long's role and wrote of him and two other informants as ideal collaborators: "One is at a loss what to praise most in them—their immense fund of knowledge or the keenness and interest they manifested in the work" (p. 9).

# Foreword

Yet he also made demeaning judgments about his chief informant that did nothing to improve understanding of Cherokee sacred formulas or of West Long as a collaborator and master of Cherokee learning (pp. 109ff.). Olbrechts's portrayal is regarded as a scholarly scandal by those familiar with the episode, and Witthoft (1948: 358) characterizes it as libelous. The published comments are impossible to justify, particularly because they dealt with a highly literate person. Olbrechts's pretense to disguise the identity of living informants by using only their initials would have failed in any case because the community was so small, but it is mind-boggling that he published their initials under their photographs.

Ethnologists have always approached the peoples with whom they work with a mixture of arrogance and diffidence. To invade community life and disrupt domestic routines for alien purposes is an arrogance. To record cultural property and carry it away in field notes or on tape is a peculiar form of plagiarism. The best ethnologists and other social scientists have tempered their presumption with a degree of humility and consideration for those with whom they work and upon whom they depend, taking pains to protect the privacy of communities and persons. Would that Olbrechts had adhered to these standards.

By the time I came under West Long's tutelage in the mid-1930s, *The Swimmer Manuscript* had been published, and its hurtful gossip was in the hands of the very people whom it depicted. Despite this bitter experience, however, West Long was willing to cooperate with other inquiring scholars, notably Frank G. Speck, and his participation as the chief intermediary and recorder in the study presented here was unreserved. Certainly this monograph would be a different and lesser work but for West Long's signal contribution.

*Leonard Broom*

Santa Barbara, California

(xx)

# PREFACE TO THE FIRST EDITION

OBSERVATIONS OF Eastern Cherokee dances and ceremonials were begun casually by Frank G. Speck in 1913 and were resumed in 1922
while he was working on the Catawba for the Bureau of American
Ethnology.[1] His chief informant, Mrs. Samson Owl, was married to a
Cherokee leader and lived with her husband's people. As the pros-
pects for continuing work among the Catawba faded with the death
of informants, Speck turned to Cherokee research and profited from
friendships with Cherokee gained during the Catawba investigation.

Subsequently, annual visits were made beginning in 1928 and continuing through 1929, 1930, and 1931, under appropriations from the
American Council of Learned Societies on the recommendation of
Dr. Franz Boas. In the winter of 1934-1935, while extending a comparative study of the religious practices of the Indians of eastern
North America, sponsored by the Faculty Research Committee of the
University of Pennsylvania, Dr. Speck returned to the Cherokee with
his son, Frank Staniford Speck, who had built a portable apparatus
for making disk recordings. Specimens of all the dance songs known
to West Long and several other elderly men of the Big Cove band
were obtained. At this time fifty songs were recorded on twenty-five

---

[1] To avoid redundancy, this preface has been slightly abridged.

# Preface

composition rubber disks, and in December and January, 1935-1936, eighteen songs were taken on twenty-two disks. The collection includes some duplicates and has not been checked with the fifteen dictaphone records of dance songs and formulas made by Dr. Frans M. Olbrechts for the Bureau of American Ethnology (Mooney and Olbrechts, 1932, p. 155). Duplications of such material, however, will never be superfluous. The records were placed in the hands of Dr. George Herzog for transcription and musicological analysis, and it is expected that he will present a work supplementary to the present study.

Leonard Broom worked at Cherokee in 1935 and 1936, under a grant from the Duke University Research Committee, and in 1940, accompanied by Gretchan Cooke Broom, he returned to make further studies and photographs. His interest in problems of acculturation first directed his attention to the Booger Dance, a striking instance of reaction against European intrusion. Subsequently, his interest broadened to include all the surviving dance lore. The convergent interests of the authors led to this collaboration.

Between 1937 and 1944 the senior author made a series of field trips to the Cherokee, for which the Faculty Research Fund of the University of Pennsylvania gave financial support. In the winter of 1944 the work was continued through subvention from the Faculty Research Fund of the University of Pennsylvania Museum with the assistance of Robert Riggs, W. S. Hadlock, and J. G. Witthoft. We have benefited also from the subsequent field work of Mr. Witthoft, conducted under grants from the Anthropology Research Fund of the University of Pennsylvania.

The diagrams of dance formations and movements were prepared at the University of California, Los Angeles, by Miss Arminta Neal, and her work is appreciatively acknowledged. Others who have aided in the tasks of cultural preservation are Dr. MacEdward Leach, Mr. Louis J. Korn, Mr. John Caldwalader, Mr. John Cotter, and Mr. S. W.

# Preface

Pennypacker II of the University of Pennsylvania, Mr. Benjamin T. Kurtz, Dr. C. E. Schaeffer, and Mr. Jack Gloyne. Dr. Arthur R. Kelly has kindly permitted the use of notes of his field work in 1929 on masks and rites. Acknowledgments are also due to Mr. and Mrs. C. T. Lloyd of Cherokee Lodge for their hospitality and aid in obtaining specimens and to Dr. H. W. Foght, formerly Superintendent of the Cherokee Agency. Finally, we are grateful to Mrs. Mary Worthington Schaeffer for assistance in editing the final draft, to Miss Genevieve Rogers for preparing the manuscript for the press, and to Mr. Witthoft for reading galley proof.

The collections of ethnological objects described and illustrated in the study made during the course of field work on the reservation have, for the most part, been placed in the University Museum, University of Pennsylvania. Some of the material is in the Denver Art Museum, Denver, Colorado; the Peabody Museum, Salem, Massachusetts; and the Museum of the American Indian (Heye Foundation), New York. A series of masks collected by Speck may be found at the Museum of the Cherokee Indian, Cherokee, North Carolina. A few masks collected by Broom are at Duke University.

West Long's elder sister Roxy, his elder half brother Lawyer Calhoun (see Pl. XXII), and his wife Mary were among the consultants and collaborators. Deliski Climbing Bear also contributed much to the study. A collection of a score of notebooks containing West Long's records in Sequoya's Cherokee script are in the archive collection of the University Museum of the University of Pennsylvania. They cover topics ranging from medical formulas to personal chronicles, and comprise the most important single body of known Cherokee materials as yet untranslated. West Long sustained the unbroken tradition of Cherokee ceremony as practiced by his group in Big Cove—the settlement that resisted European cultural intrusions and preserved its ceremonial heritage more effectively than other groups or towns of the Eastern band.

# Preface

The present reservation in Swain and Jackson counties, North Carolina, comprises five town settlements or localized groups: Yellow Hill, Wolf Town, Bird Town, Paint Town, and Big Cove. These local precincts, some of which bear the names of former sib (or clan) divisions, have been associated tentatively by James Mooney (1888, p. 247) with the "mother towns" of the old nation. Differences have been noted in some cultural details pertaining to these groups which call for closer study. Among other aspects of rivalry, they form opposed units in the Ball Game ceremonies.

The Big Cove band boast of never having ceased their native dancing. West Long himself, in his later years, was a mentor and leader in the performances. He is cited as one of the active informants with whom Olbrechts studied in preparing his monograph on the Swimmer Manuscript (Olbrechts, 1929; Mooney and Olbrechts, 1932). Olbrechts' important contributions to our knowledge of Cherokee protective and curative practices, and those of Mooney (1890a, 1890b, 1891, 1900) should be consulted carefully in connection with the present essay.

We have not attempted to correlate the preliminary notations published by Gilbert (1943).

*F.G.S.*
and
*L.B.*

Philadelphia
and
Los Angeles

# CHEROKEE DANCE AND DRAMA

# I.

# Introduction

THERE is no doubt that the Cherokee are among the best-known Indian tribes. The exceptional rapidity with which they took over the technology and ideas of Europeans and the continuous pressure on their frontiers from the sixteenth century have been common literary coin for a century. The invention by Sequoya of his syllabary, which made a literate people of his tribesmen, added luster to Cherokee ethnohistory. So thoroughly did the Cherokee change that they became known as one of the Five Civilized Tribes of the Southeast. Historians have dwelt upon the early wars of the Cherokee, their intrigues with the French, their coming to grips with the settlers of Tennessee, Georgia, and the Carolinas, the tragic event of the Removal, and the experiences of the Western band in Indian Territory. In short, the Cherokee people have received much attention from both popular and technical writers, and the Cherokee nation looms large in the bibliography of American ethnohistory, missionary activity, treaty negotiation, and sentiment. But systematic ethnological studies of the people have been relatively few, considering the wealth of other work.

The ethnology of the Cherokee has been so little investigated that Cherokee culture is known chiefly for its acquisitions from white civilization rather than for its native properties. In this study we have undertaken the task of covering one part of this deficiency. We have attempted to describe in detail the surviving forms of dance and ritual as practiced among the Eastern band of Cherokee and especially among the Big Cove group during the past two decades. The record thus accumulated was made too late for us to achieve a full and rounded account of Cherokee ceremonial life, yet it is sufficient to warrant some historical comparisons and it is certain that the speed with which the aboriginal culture is fading makes this a more adequate record than could be secured even now.

The general attributes of the culture of the Southeastern tribes are too near the horizon of a civilization—a simple one, to be sure—for us to find in their ceremonial exhibitions the intensity and the individual magic that one expects in the religious and public rituals of peoples of the marginal cultural types. In technology the Cherokee operate on a level decidedly above the simple hunting stage. Their ritual has lost some of the primitive flavor of simple symbolism, and aesthetic elements seem to have developed, at least so far as dance performances are concerned. In the combined dance and drama, obscured religious motives are undoubtedly present, but they are no more important than artistic conventions. Surely they are less important in the direct consciousness of the participants and spectators than are the aesthetic and the dramatic elements. It is our impression from observations over a period of years that Cherokee rites exhibit a definite consciousness of dramatic gesture, which reaches its peak in the performance of the Booger Dance, and this dramatic quality seems to us more evident than in the dance rites of the Iroquois.

While the Eastern Cherokee as a whole occupy the position of a marginal montane people in the Southeastern culture zone, the Big Cove subgroup, with whom we have been concerned almost exclusively, is again marginal within Eastern Cherokee culture. Theirs is a terrain of chilly mountain slopes, conifer-shaded ravines, and cold torrents, where severe winters shorten the growing season. These con-

# Introduction

ditions and a former abundance of animal resources molded the economy of a relatively sparse mountain population in a fashion different from the settlements in the more favored bottom lands. That the Big Cove settlement preserved more of the old-time life of the Cherokee natives is assumed by all students. But isolation alone may not account for cultural persistence.

More is to be found in the Booger Dance drama at Big Cove than a cultural form persisting in a geographical pocket. In this dance, which stands in sharp contrast to the others, we have a record of the anxieties of a people, their reactions against the symbol of the invader, and their insecurity in their dealings with the white man. In general, the dances reveal an equilibrium between the Cherokee and their environment, both animate and inanimate. In the Booger Dance the equilibrium is precarious. We make bold to interpret its function in this way: by relating the invasion of the white man to the spiritual forces of nature with which the Cherokee aboriginally learned to cope, the potency of the threat is somehow lessened. This is truly an anachronism, for the Cherokee come to feel more secure in dealing with a strange physical reality when they are able to transmute it into a familiar ritual context. With the white invaders as men they cannot deal, but with the white invaders disguised as mythical animals and frivolous demimen they feel competent to deal. The reader will want to bear these comments in mind in reviewing the ceremonial descriptions.

In presenting this material we have a kind of moral problem to face. Like all outsiders coming to the Cherokee, in truth like the prototypes of the Boogers themselves, we often appear in their midst uninvited, seeking something to exploit. Like the Boogers, with unmannerly insistence we ethnologists break into Cherokee home circles at the height of their social festivities. Politely these people tolerate our intrusion until, our desires gratified, we depart. As Wulf Sachs puts it: "Only a probing into the depths of the human mind, into the wide

( 3 )

range of desires, conflicts, strivings, contradictory and confusing, can give understanding. And if this applies to the study of those whose language, habits, and daily life are identical with ours, how much more careful must we be in dealing with those who live in entirely different surroundings, who are strangers to us, and whom we approach usually with either marked hostility or unconscious aversion, or with sentimental idealization and studied friendliness."[1]

We can look back somewhat differently, however, upon our intrusion into the privacies of Cherokee society. Only a free coöperation on the part of our collaborator, West Long, enabled us to accomplish the task of putting on record this repertory of songs and dances. Although West Long is now dead, some part of his extensive knowledge of festivities and rituals is preserved in a literature bearing his name as its primary source. This accomplishment is what he desired for his people and himself. We lament the fact that West Long's death occurred before he had the gratification of seeing his knowledge in print. Parts of the discussion, however, had been completed and read to him in his mountain cabin, and the descriptions of all the dance proceedings had been checked and corrected by him over the long period of preparation. He was pleased that his name should appear as their sponsor, and he knew from the beginning that he would be a collaborator in the final record of his people's drama. His reward, aside from the honorariums he received as an informant, was to preserve the tradition of Cherokee ceremonies.

We do not regard our heavy dependence on one informant as a weakness. The very nature of Cherokee dances and their organization at Big Cove make the method a necessity and, in this instance, the necessity a virtue. The dance is, to be sure, an aspect of social life that represents the action of a group, not of an individual. But West Long was a leader, an authority, as a priest would be in a rite. The people, at least in this late stage of acculturation, are the laity, not

---

[1] For notes to chapter 1 see page 99.

# Introduction

unlike the mannikins of a performance who play their parts under the manipulations of their master. Cherokee ritual dance performance includes some of the aims of a dramatic exhibition. It is only from the leaders—the self-appointed cult of the learned—that deeper meanings and spiritual motives may be discovered, as Dr. Olbrechts found in his study of medicine song formulas and medicine men.[2] The wise men of the dance songs and the dance singers and leaders appear to be also the medicine men, for those chiefly responsible for Cherokee survivals are not narrow specialists in aboriginal lore. West Long himself was an example of this bilateral profession.

We have dealt here only with the rites in song, those performed in connection with the dances, and some of the chants used in hunting. The series of dance songs is more complete for the Big Cove group than the hunting songs that were collected and recorded as chance offered; but the hunting songs are interesting because of their strong magical content. To increase the hunting song series will require more intensive inquiry and wider travel among the people, since hunting songs often prove to be individual heritages and may be purchased. The entire song series, nevertheless,—both these and the dance songs that are a social property free to be acquired by anyone—constitutes a conceptual unit so far as origin and function are concerned. They were explained by West Long as emanating from one source, bequeathed to the Cherokee as spiritualistic aids in their struggle for life against an adverse animal kingdom, the agency of disease, and a menacing world of mankind.[3]

Although it is easy to compile highly modified Biblical tales in the guise of Cherokee myths, the ceremonies themselves seem to have been little modified by Western influences. However, we have not attempted in this paper to explore in detail the influences of European dances on the Cherokee forms. This, rather, seems to be the proper task for a specialist on the eighteenth-century colonial dance. If any such changes have occurred, they have been sufficiently integrated with the aboriginal forms to present an uninterrupted façade. We do, however, suggest the analysis of Western elements as a worth-while and interesting problem.

A much more important effect of European competition has been a direct attack on the practice of the dance and the prestige of its participants. From the beginning of missionary contact early in the nineteenth century until the present, both native and white religious workers among the Cherokee have regarded the dances as competitive systems and treated them as curious practices of ignorant savages to be derided, as symptoms of idolatrous behavior to be challenged, or as a system of decadent revelry and a focus of infection for the forces of sin equated with the forces of intemperance. Reflecting this are the following: "Clauder [a Moravian missionary, 1837] notes that even some of the 'veterans of the ball ground and all-night dance' are becoming concerned about spiritual things,"[4] and " . . . if heathen Cherokees could raise $3,500 in bets at a ball game, Christian Indians certainly might . . . bring an offering to the Lord."[5] Elias Boudinot as editor of the Cherokee *Phoenix* also betrays the missionary attitude of the period.

Today, with the passing of the last great leaders, the most vigorous assaults are being made by Cherokee preachers who manifest their fundamentalist precepts in attacking the remnants of the aboriginal culture. Cherokee ceremonials would disappear soon, in any event, out of sheer growth of ignorance and loss of interest, but this energetic attack from within strikes at the self-confidence of the leaders, reduces their prestige with possible participants, and surely hastens the day when the ribaldry of the Booger Dance and the solemnity of the Green Corn Dance will no longer be known. The preservation of superficial aspects of the dances adapted for the entertainment, if not the edification, of tourists will do little to postpone this event.

In some cultures of eastern North America, change has taken place in the religious significance of dances, tending toward the profanation

# Introduction

of ritual even within the era of ethnological observation. As a result, the dramatic and exhibitional qualities of dances have eclipsed their symbolic and magical value. To what degree a formerly greater sanctity may have been present in the Cherokee dance is difficult to say. Cherokee animal dances are now mainly social forms. It is intimated, however, that in former times, when animals were real factors in native life, the dances named for them possessed more meaning as signatory magic. Among the more sophisticated Cherokee and those whites who approve their retention as a valued tradition, we find them regarded as folk dances. But older people and those who are inclined to be credulous in religious matters believe that the dances exert an influence over animals and their associations with man.

The Cherokee year aboriginally consisted irregularly of twelve or thirteen months because of confusion of solar and lunar calendars. Functionally, the year was punctuated by six festivals symbolizing several essential phases of Cherokee life; the seasonal limitations on some of the surviving dances may reflect the periodicity of aboriginal ceremony.[6]

There was anciently a regular series of festivals—six in all—and each with significant peculiarities. These were held in the national heptagon, when the entire population of the seven clans assembled under the summons of the *leku* (high priest) through his seven councillors, by whom the ceremonials were directed: and here, being the metropolis, every abode on such occasions was open, and every hospitality gratuitous. Minor festivals were also celebrated every new moon—more especially at the beginning of each quarter of the year;—as well as a regular sacrifice on every seventh day. Occasional festivals were also mentioned; the most remarkable of which took place in remote times, once in seven years.

The six great festivals were observed in the following order:

1st. The festival of the first new moon of spring, which was celebrated about the time the grass began to grow.[7]

2nd. *Sah,looh,stu-knee, keeh steh steeh;* a preliminary or new green-corn feast, held when the young corn first became fit to taste.

( 7 )

# Cherokee Dance and Drama

3rd. *Tung,nah, kaw,* HOONGH-*ni;* mature or ripe green-corn festival, which succeeded the other in some forty or fifty days, when the corn had become hard and perfect.[8]

4th. *Nung,tah,-tay-quah;* great new-moon feast, which occurred on the occasion of the appearance of the first new moon of autumn.[9]

5th. *Ah,tawh,hung,nah;* propitiation or cementation festival, succeeding the former in about ten days.[10]

6th. *Eelah,wahtah,lay-kee;* the festival of the exulting or bounding bush, which came somewhat later.

Another pre-Removal commentary conveys a remarkable amount of flavor and information as well as a perspective of missionary attitudes.[11]

The conversation commenced by one of the young ladies inquiring "if the Cherokees were idolaters."

*Cornelia.* Properly speaking they are not idolaters: yet before the missionaries instructed them they were totally ignorant of the true character of Jehovah. They knew nothing of Christ; and were universally superstitious; consulting witches, conjurers, and other wicked persons upon the most trivial occasions.

*Jerome.* What kind of beings are conjurers?

*Cornelia.* Indian conjurers are generally called *medicine men,* and rank next to the chiefs. They are consulted with great ceremony, by all descriptions of persons, and are accounted to be very powerful; formerly, there were annual festivals, in which the conjurers bore a very conspicuous part.

*Delia.* Please to describe some of their festivals.

*Cornelia.* They used to have one when the corn was in the milk, before they tasted it; on these occasions, there was a general meeting of all the inhabitants of the district or village, and, after all were assembled, the conjurer took the kernels from seven ears of corn, and after burning them in the fire, with many foolish ceremonies, the whole company were allowed to feast upon *roasted corn,* and eat it in their cabins, after they went home. Before eating the green bean, they go over the same ceremony. When the corn gets hard, they have another frolic called the *green corn dance,* which lasts several days. In March, they used to have a yearly frolic called making *new fire.*

*Talbot.* How is this performed?

( 8 )

# Introduction

*Cornelia.* They meet, and dance all night. In the morning, the fire is produced by drilling a dried grape vine; it takes the conjurer, and seven men, to accomplish this work—everybody puts out every spark of fire in his dwelling, and comes to this, and receives the new. The *physic dance* is going out of fashion now, but it was once in high repute. It is the province of females to manage all the ceremonies of this dance, excepting the services of seven men, who bring the water to boil the medicine, and to carry it when boiled to every person present, to drink of it, which is never done before a person ascends the top of a building called the *town house*, and sings a song; the house is previously painted with white clay; the dance is continued seven days; and they are obliged to continue it two nights out of the seven; after bathing, and drinking a small quantity of the physic, they all disperse. I suppose I have told you enough about conjurers.

*Jerome.* O no, cousin; do tell us all you ever heard.

*Cornelia.* Why it would take me till midnight; and when heard, would do you no real good.

*Talbot.* But do tell us more; perhaps it will make us pity their ignorance, and be more willing to give money to enlighten them.

*Cornelia.* If I thought it would have that effect, I would tell conjurer and witch stories till day-break. I will mention one or two more frolics. One is called *making rain;* another, the *eagle tail* dance. While the conjurer is about making it rain, seven men, or seven women, who represent the seven clans, into which the Cherokee nation is divided, fast till the rain begins to fall; then the tongue of a deer is sacrificed. During this whole time, the conjurer fasts; and when he speaks, he utters words incomprehensible to all but a *few* who have been instructed with the design of following the same practices.

*Andrew.* I long to hear about the *eagle tail* dance.

*Cornelia.* That is designed to inculcate a warlike spirit in the young. When a large assembly have convened, the old warriors rehearse, in the dance, their former "deeds of noble daring"; the dangers and deaths they have encountered; and the victories they have won. At day-break, the boys partake of some slight refreshment; they go out to meet the young men, who set themselves in battle array against the boys, and after pelting each other most heartily with mud, they retire.

*Jerome.* Are conjurers of no other use?

*Cornelia.* In seasons of sickness, when any epidemic prevails, no person feels safe until the conjurer has rendered him invulnerable to the disease.

( 9 )

# Cherokee Dance and Drama

*Jerome.* How can he do that?

*Cornelia.* He cannot; but the deluded heathens think he can.

*Delia.* What does he do?

*Cornelia.* He first selects seven men to go out and hunt until they have taken seven deer, which are to be carried to a particular place; he then orders them to retire to the woods fasting, and gather a variety of roots and herbs, and place them with the deer, in the mean time, fasting himself; he puts the herbs into a large pot, and keeps them boiling till every person desirous of escaping the contagion assembles, the deer being caught, roasted in haste, and eaten by the multitude. At night every female, old and young, dances round a large fire seven times, to the music of a drum made of a keg, or old pan. The old conjurer sits all the night over his pot of herbs, to prevent their ceasing to boil a moment. At day-break, the whole assembly dance with great zeal till sunrise; then each person partakes of the conjurer's dose, washes his body in a small quantity of the liquor; then the pot is again replenished with fresh herbs, and seven men are selected to stay by, and keep it boiling seven days longer, refraining from food each day till sunset. At the end of seven days, the assembly breaks up, every family being careful to carry away a portion of the liquor. After seven days more, they all return, and go over the same ceremonies seven days, they then go home fearless of the distemper, and rejoicing in the skill and power of the conjurer.

*Jerome.* Do they always succeed in preserving from disease?

*Cornelia.* No; but when they fail, it is easy to satisfy the deluded multitude; on one occasion, the measles prevailed, and the conjurers failed to check their progress.

*Jerome.* How did they pacify the people?

*Cornelia.* By telling them that the missionaries prevented the success of their charms.

*Jerome.* Are the conjurers paid for their labor?

*Cornelia.* Yes; they receive the skins of the deer, and a string of white beads from every family whom they render proof against the distemper.

*Delia.* How do they cure the sick?

*Cornelia.* It is feared, they as often kill as cure. A woman sent for Dr. Butlar, who was very successful in relieving her, and she seemed in a fine way to recover; but one day feeling rather more unwell, her friends persuaded her to have an Indian doctor, who directed her to be put into a place so hot, that immediately she was in a profuse perspiration; while in this state, they plunged her into the river, which caused her death in a short time.

( 10 )

# Introduction

*Delia.* Are witches as troublesome as conjurers?

*Cornelia.* They often murder persons, whom they suppose to be witches. Mr. Hoyt found in his visits a miserable woman, and her little son, whose whole family had been murdered for this supposed crime. They were in the family of a native Christian, who fed and clothed them, and attempted to learn them to read, and instructed them in Christian duties.

*Mrs. Claiborne.* What are the most prominent Indian vices at present?

*Cornelia.* I believe intoxication, Sabbath-breaking, and evils arising from immodesty, are at present the most conspicuous.

To return to current observations, the manner of conducting and participating in dances gives little indication of ulterior motives beyond what has been pointed out. The dances and songs are regarded as a bequest of the sacrificed Stone Coat monster to assuage the ills of humanity. The common designation Stone Coat or Friendship Dance carries this idea.

The animal and social dances comprise a grouping or block performed in an evening's program. It is initiated by the Beginning Dance (p. 65) and is concluded by the Round or Running Dance (p. 68). The other dances are performed between these two in any order desired by the sponsors, except that the Corn Dance (p. 77) must be held toward morning rather than in the earlier part of the night.

Although those Cherokee dances that may be called rites are likely to be performed in either summer or winter, the majority of the animal or social dances may be called at any time.

The winter dances, the Booger, Eagle, and Bear dances, associated with ghosts, the defunct, and arbitrarily with certain animals, are supposed to be given during times of frost, lest they affect the growth of vegetation by attracting cold and death. The summer dances, the Green Corn and Ballplayers' dances, are associated with crops and vegetation. The remainder may be performed freely, usually on Saturdays, at the home of a member of the Big Cove community.

# Cherokee Dance and Drama

Ordinarily, these dances are prompted only by the desire for social intercourse and entertainment.

Special occasions, however, call for an assembly, such as the Burial Dance referred to by Mooney and Olbrechts. This was practiced in the Big Cove in West Long's time. The Burial Dance takes place at the home of the deceased for the purpose of alleviating the grief of the bereaved family and turning their thoughts again to the normal affairs of life. It lasts for seven successive nights after the death. One may observe a correspondence here with the condolence ceremonies of the linguistically related Iroquois. Mooney and Olbrechts refer to the burial series as the most impressive, lengthy, and poetic of all Cherokee ceremonies.[12]

In the ceremonial dance series the allegorical drama is a chief feature. Its objective is the benefit of the community, and the action is carried out by a volunteer company, not by any esoteric group, society, sib, or family. Participation is open even to strangers and aliens. Performances are symbolic of amity and hostility, intercourse, animal pantomime of pursuit and hunting. They are placative in purpose and illustrative of myth and a cosmic outlook. Collectively, the songs may be conceived as medicine to prevent affliction or to provide immunity. The evil potencies against which they are directed are innate in animals, plants, human beings, and ghosts. Finally, they provide social gatherings for amusement and diversion in a small and isolated community of agriculturists and hunters in a mountain environment.

The dances may have tangental historical connection with the legend of the Seven Dancing Boys Who Became Transformed into Stars, the widely known Pleiades fable. The version of the tale reported here as narrated by West Long is close to that current in Cayuga Iroquois and Delaware-Munsee mythology, although the story is not specifically associated with the origin of dancing in the Cherokee tradition.

# Introduction

THE DANCING BOYS AND THE ORIGIN OF THE SEVEN STARS (PLEIADES)

There were once seven boys who used to spend all their time dancing. They did nothing but dance around in a circle with their drum. Their parents tried to induce them to stop but they did not obey. They kept on dancing. One time their parents decided to do something about it. They went to force them to stop. As they got near the dancing place they saw the boys rising in the air. And so they rose into the sky dancing, and are there now. The smallest star is said by some to be the drum, but others think this star is only the smallest of the boys.[18]

## ORIGIN OF DANCE SONGS AND FORMULAS

According to Cherokee tradition, all tribal chanting, for whatever purpose, originated from a mythical event—the slaying and sacrifice of a monster creature called Stone Coat (in Cherokee, nã'ʸyũ'nũwĭ', literally, "stone coat-on"). The same origin tale accounts for the entire series of song compositions known to the people "since before the time of Christ," as West Long put it. It accounts for the songs that govern the dances, those chanted to further the Cherokee in their dealings with game animals and birds, cultivated plants, and wild medicinal herbs; and also the man-animal opponent, or enemy, in games, in war and in peace, and in social contacts. It is the legendary rationale in love-making, protection against witchcraft, economic competition, and even in such peripheral events as tribal or racial contacts. A free rendering of the legend is given in the following version by West Long.

### LEGEND OF STONE COAT
#### HIS SACRIFICE AND THE BEQUEST OF MEDICINE DANCES AND SONG FORMULAS TO THE CHEROKEE

Long ago a creature lived among the people in human form whose name was Stone Coat. In his natural state he was covered completely with scaly armor sufficient to protect him from any attack—an invincible monster. When he lived among the people no one knew his identity. Furthermore, he could make himself invisible at will. And he went from place to place wherever the people did not suspect him, killing them as often as he needed food, in order to secure their livers. For human livers were his sustenance.

Finally he came to a Cherokee village where he took the form of a little lost orphan boy. The man who found him took pity on him and brought him home to raise. One morning, soon after, one of this man's children was found dead. They examined the body and found that its liver had been taken out. Such a sorrowful event caused deep sorrow in the village, for this was the first time that anyone had died. They consulted the medicine man to find out what could be done. Some of the people wanted to take immediate action to discover and punish the supposed killer. The medicine man advised them to wait, lest they make a mistake, and see what would happen next to guide them in taking the wisest action. No one suspected the poor orphan boy of having anything to do with the deed. For a few days nothing happened. Then one morning another child was found dead from the same cause. Although they had kept watch to see if anyone had entered the settlement, no intruder had been discovered. And so when they took council over the curse of death which had come upon them it was decided that someone among their own people was the cause. They feared that the children and finally the grown people would be killed for their livers and all perish unless the cause could be found and removed.

When another of his children had been killed in the same manner, the man who had adopted the orphan boy suspected the boy of the deed. He noticed that he had no appetite for regular food after the death of each child. So he went to the council of chiefs and medicine men who were now holding serious meetings to determine what might be done for relief, and told them of his suspicions. Some advised that they attack and slay the boy at once. But others advised caution, saying that he must be a powerful spirit in disguise and that to attack him outright might result in failure, arousing his anger and causing him to destroy them all. They finally agreed to lie in wait to watch him, that the medicine men might divine some means by which he could be disposed of without danger. He was so very powerful that it was thought best to allow the death of a few more children before they took final action.

At length one of the medicine men declared in council that he had found a way to entrap and slay the killer. He ordered that they secure the aid of seven women whose menstrual period came at the full of the moon, so that they might lie in wait along the path taken by the killer in his journeys to and fro across the mountains in search of victims. For he had discovered that this was one way to weaken and destroy the killer. The women were found and the plan carried out. They lay along the path where the victim was supposed to come, with their legs uncovered. When Stone Coat, who was the killer in disguise, came by he saw them and said, "Well, well! Beautiful women." Then all at once he felt queer, began to vomit blood and grow weak. As soon as he passed each woman he vomited more blood, finally becoming so weak that he lay down, unable to move. Then the people who had been waiting for the results came to where he lay stretched upon the ground, to see the dying Stone Coat.

Stone Coat then, knowing he was about to die, said, "Cause as many of the people as can possibly come to gather about this place. Build a fire [of basswood fagots, the narrator later added] around me and burn me up." It was done as he commanded and the Cherokee came from distances to witness the sacrifice. When they lighted the fire Stone Coat began to talk to them, telling them that while he was burning and the smoke and smell of his burning flesh arose toward the sky, there would issue forth a series of songs. These, he told them, were his offering to the people to aid them in all branches of life. As the songs came forth, he commanded, they were to learn them and teach them to their children, to be used forever by the Cherokee.

The dying Stone Coat also told them that if they had tried to kill him by force in the beginning they would have failed because it was ordained that they should not have relief until they had learned what suffering was. Knowing the depths of suffering and the joy of relief, he said, would make them value the songs they were now to learn and the medicine they were to gain by his death and sacrifice. He said, "You kill me, so I leave disease in the world behind me. But my songs will cure that." He also told them that besides leaving with them the magic songs for dances in fulfillment of their social life, and the song formulas, he would leave them a quantity of powerful medicines in the form of pieces of stone forming his stone coat, which would be found in the ashes after the fire had consumed his body.

Then they burned his body and watched him all night. He kept on singing different songs all the time he was burning, until he died, when he became silent. Then as his spirit arose to the sky in the morning, the singing still came forth and could be heard until out of hearing in the highness. And the people, gathered around the sacrifice, learned all the songs. Some they employed for dancing when they were all together and others were used by people alone for hunting, for war, and other purposes, as medicine. After the ascent of Stone Coat's spirit they examined the ashes and found pieces of stone all broken up by the heat of the fire. These were the particles of his stone coat. All the men gathered up the pieces. And as each took a piece of the stone he decided what line of life he would follow. Some decided to be bear hunters, some deer hunters, some buffalo hunters, some fishermen; others chose to be handsome for women. And whatever pursuit was chosen and followed became the life calling of the people and their descendants, with the songs and medicine for each purpose in life.

Some additional explanatory comments were subsequently elicited. Emphasis was laid upon the belief that there was no disease in the world before the time of Stone Coat, and that death originated through him. When the monster approached his victim he would transform himself into an old woman whose forefinger was sharp and hooked. She would offer to delouse the victim and during the process would puncture his skull and then hook out and eat his liver.

A variant version of his downfall relates that all attempts to slay the creature were in vain. A small bird (the tufted titmouse, *Baeolophus bicolor,* was the identified variety in the narration) agreed to betray the monster's only vulnerable part. The bird lit on his hand and they aimed their shafts there. But it was a lie and Stone Coat was not killed. They caught the bird and split his tongue. It has remained so to this time. Next the chickadee (*Penthestes atricapillus*) offered to make the betrayal and they believed him. He alighted on Stone Coat's palm. They aimed there and the wound was fatal. Such flagrant legendary inconsistencies will not disturb the sense of the tale.

For comparison we quote in full the version recorded by Mooney between 1887 and 1890.[14]

### NUN'YUNU'WI, THE STONE MAN

Once, when all the people of the settlement were out in the mountains on a great hunt, one man who had gone on ahead climbed to the top of a high ridge and found a large river on the other side. While he was looking across he saw an old man walking about on the opposite ridge, with a cane that seemed to be made of some bright, shining rock. The hunter watched and saw that every little while the old man would point his cane in a certain direction, then draw it back and smell the end of it. At last he pointed it in the direction of the hunting camp on the other side of the mountain, and this time when he drew back the staff he sniffed it several times, as if it smelled very good, and then started along the ridge straight for the camp. He moved very slowly, with the help of the cane, until he reached the end of the ridge, when he threw the cane out into the air and it became a bridge of shining rock stretching across the river. After he had crossed over the bridge it became a cane again, and the old man picked it up and started over the mountain toward the camp.

The hunter was frightened and felt sure that it meant mischief, so he hurried on down the mountain and took the shortest trail back to the camp, to get there before the old man. When he got there and told his story the medicine-man said the old man was a wicked cannibal monster called Nun'yunu'wi, "Dressed in Stone," who lived in that part of the country and was always going about the mountains looking for some hunter to kill and eat. It was very hard to escape from him, because his stick guided him like a dog, and it was nearly as hard to kill him, because his whole body was covered with a skin of solid rock. If he came he would kill and eat them all, and there was only one way to save themselves. He could not bear to look upon a menstrual woman, and if they could find seven menstrual women to stand in the path as he came along, the sight would kill him.

So they asked among all the women and found seven who were sick in that way, and with one of them it had just begun. By the order of the medicine-man they stripped themselves and stood along the path where the old man would come. Soon they heard Nun'yunu'wi coming through the woods, feeling his way with his stone cane. He came along the trail to where the first woman was standing, and as soon as he saw her he started and cried out: "Yu! my grandchild; you are in a very bad state!" He hurried past her, but in a moment he met the next woman, and cried out again: "Yu! my child; you are in a terrible way," and hurried past her, but now he was vomiting blood. He hurried on and met the third and the fourth and the fifth woman, but with each one that he saw his step grew weaker until, when he came to the last one, with whom the sickness had just begun, the blood poured from his mouth and he fell down on the trail.

Then the medicine-man drove seven sourwood stakes through his body and pinned him to the ground, and when night came they piled great logs

( 17 )

over him and set fire to him, and all the people gathered around to see. Nun'yunu'wi was a great ada'we-hi and knew many secrets, and now as the fire came close to him he began to talk, and told them the medicine for all kinds of sickness. At midnight he began to sing, and sang the hunting songs for calling up the bear and the deer and all the animals of the woods and mountains. As the blaze grew hotter his voice sank lower and lower, until at last, when daylight came, the logs were a heap of white ashes and the voice was still.

Then the medicine-man told them to rake off the ashes, and where the body had lain they found only a large lump of red wa'di paint and a magic u'lunsu'ti stone. He kept the stone for himself, and calling the people around him he painted them, on face and breast, with the red wa'di, and whatever each person prayed for while the painting was being done—whether for hunting success, for working skill, or for a long life—that gift was his.

Olbrechts noted that the medicine men were losing the accounts of the origins of the sacred formulas and songs. The origins are merely referred to as something passed on from "the people who lived a long time ago." Olbrechts says: "... sporadically a medicine man will attribute the Cherokee's knowledge of formulas and prescriptions to a revelation of the Apportioner, ... the Creator as preached by Christian missionaries. The same man on another occasion will tell you, with just as honest a conviction, that 'the people inherited the knowledge from a powerful wizard when he died,' referring to Stone-clad's death."[15]

# 2.

# The Repertory of Dances

THE purposes of the dance rites bear some functional similarities to the specifically medicinal formulas reported by Mooney and Olbrechts. The medical formulas are the private properties of medicine men; the dance rites are social and communal, free to all and for the benefit of all. The medical formulas exist to cure maladies and afflictions already manifested in symptoms among sufferers; the dance rites are prophylactic. The principles that insure individual health and social welfare (collective and individual well-being) are inculcated in the dances. The dramatic but friendly mimicry of various animals and certain human beings has an effect of "magically" immunizing the sources, according to native reasoning. The benefits of social intercourse fostered by the dance festivals are also apparent.

The host who sponsors the dance gathering at his home and issues oral invitations has no further ceremonial duties, except as noted in the Booger Dance (p. 25).

The Driver (the designation has become a Cherokee family name) is appointed by the host to announce leaders for dances and the dance sequence, to preserve order, to urge participation in the dances, and to act as sergeant at arms. The office is honorary and for a single night. He is known as ɢaˋnǎ'wi:sti:'stǐ:, "starter, forcer [habitual]." The term also signifies a locomotive engineer. The alternative term is di:'yɛli:dɔ'hǐ:, literally "driver."

# Cherokee Dance and Drama

The leading singer, who also dances at the head of the column, is known as ikk:ā'yi:alɛ'hãski:', "standing up first [habitually]."

During the summer the dances may be held outdoors in fine weather, usually in the yard of a dwelling. The formations turn about a fire made of logs stacked on end to form a cone about 4 feet high. With the first frost the dances are moved indoors. In the center of a room cleared of furnishings is an inverted corn mortar or, as a substitute, a chair. The mortar is vaguely symbolic of economic plenty and is associated with women. This fertility connotation is from the signification of corn as "old woman" or "our mother."

Before about 1870 there was a round house for dances, called gāt'i:', in the Soco town settlement. A ledge of stones now barely discernible marks its location and it may be pointed out as one travels the road leading up Soco Creek.

Before proceeding to accounts of the dances, something should be said about the musical instruments that will be referred to repeatedly. Three principal tympanic instruments are used to accompany dance songs: a hollowed wooden water drum, ahu:'lĩ'', "it [hollow] has covering on"; a gourd hand-rattle, gɑntsɛ'ti:'', "gourd"; and box tortoise shell leg-rattles, called ɒaksi' ɒi:nãsat.t'i'', "terrapin put on legs." The leg-rattles are worn on each leg by the woman partner of the dance leader.

A typical drum was made of a section of buckeye trunk, 11 by 8 inches, hollowed by gouging to leave a 2-inch bottom, with walls averaging ½ inch thick, colored with red clay and sumach stain over the entire surface. The head was a woodchuck skin held down by a hickory hoop ¾ inch wide. There was a perforation on the lower part to drain water when the drum was not in use. On one side of a specimen used at Big Cove were carved two small buffaloes in high relief. The drumstick was of hickory, 15 inches long. Another drum was 13 inches long and 9 inches wide, stained bluish gray with pokeberry juice; it had no perforation for water and no decoration. Its drumstick was of hickory, 11 inches long, with a small knob on the end. An extra drumstick was of black walnut, 7 inches long.

When ready to be used, the drumhead is soaked in water, the hoop pounded down over it on the open end of the drum section until

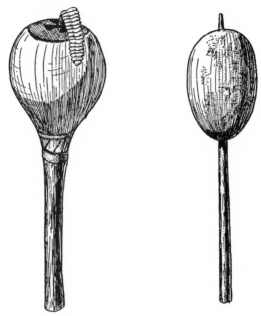

Figure 1. Gourd rattles, one, with rattlesnake rattles, used to accompany dance songs

stretched sufficiently to make it ring when struck lightly, and enough water placed in the bottom of the drum to enable the operator to remoisten the head by shaking the drum or turning it upside down. It requires some experience to tune the water drum properly and keep it resonant throughout a whole night's use.

Gourd rattles (see Pl. XV, *a*, and fig. 1) are made of hollow, dried gourds perforated at each end of the long axis. The gourd neck may be used as a handle, or a hickory-stick handle, roughly 10 inches long, may be locked in with a small hickory cotter pin. The rattle gourd is usually 4 inches long and 3 inches wide, and rarely has decorations or coloring in red or black. Sometimes the gourd is irregularly punctured with an awl to improve its tone. Examples of gourd rattles with rattle-snake rattles (see fig. 1) or hawk-feather pendants have been seen in the Bird Town settlement.

The turtle shell (*Terrapene carolina*) leg-rattles (see Pl. XI, *a*) are clusters of four or five whole shells dried so that the plastron and carapace firmly encase the pebbles. The shells are fastened to a strong cloth, roughly 11 by 12 inches, with tie strings at top and bottom for attachment just below the knee. One specimen, probably close to the aboriginal form, had five shells and four deer hoofs dangling from the top shell as rattles. The base was of woodchuck hide, 8 by 9 inches, with tie strings and fastenings of the hide. The leg-rattles are worn only by a woman, and in rare instances by two if an extra pair of rattles is available. The woman enters the dance behind the leader and produces the rattling sound only at specified passages of the song and dance. By skillful control of her movements she can hush the rattles while walking or pound out a vigorous rhythm.

The tremolo shaking of the rattle or a rapid beating of the drum is a signal for the beginning and end of song units. The tremolo is made by a vibration of the wrist with the rattle held aloft, not by a circular motion, and occurs during the song only in a stomp interval or when a leader wishes the column to reverse. The expert leader will end the tremolo by lowering his rattle until it stops.

Relevant native terms are as follows:

| | |
|---|---|
| gɑni:ˈla gɑntsɛˈti:ʹ | slow habitual rattling |
| gɑni:ˈla ahoʹli gãsti:ˈi: | slow drum beating |
| gadzɛnuˈli: gɑntsɛˈti ʹ | fast habitual rattling |
| gadzɛnuˈla gãsti:ˈi: | fast beating tremolo |

## Repertory of Dances

| | |
|---|---|
| a\`‘sɛltɔ‘ti:′ gɑntsɛ‘ti:′ | raising rattle habitually |
| di:tɔ\`hi:nɛgi: | leading by hand (i.e., changing direction, reversing) |
| ayɔ\`hi:stɔ‘ti:\`yi | stop or end |
| alɛ̃′‘tiskɑ̃i:, (or) alɛ̃′‘tɔ‘ti kanogi:skɑ̃\`i | beginning song |
| kanogi:\`to‘ (or) | habitual one song |
| dakanogi:\`to‘ | habitual plural songs (This is the main dance song section.) |
| ani:lɑ̃waliskĩ | habitual answering (plural) (This is the answering part by the dancers in response to the leader's phrases.) |

As the leader begins, he walks once counterclockwise (all movements take this direction) around the circle, shaking the rattle as he decides what songs he will perform. An apparent laxity of form is due to nothing more than the inclination and memory of individual leaders. Although the duration of an animal dance averages ten to fifteen minutes, some leaders may prolong the dance to as much as twenty minutes. The Booger Dance varies in length according to the number of masked performers, and was observed to take as long as an hour and a half when there were ten masked performers. A dance almost always deviates in some details from the form of other occasions. This may be due to the ability, mood, or caprice of the leader, and may provoke laughter by adding an unexpected element to the play. Partial intoxication, error, forgetfulness, confusion, and inexperience all add to the variation.

Even the simplest single dance unit, when complete, comprises four song periods, punctuated by the leader's signals. A characteristic instance is as follows:

1. Walking period in which the leader beats a tremolo, walks once around the dance circle, and shakes the tremolo again.

# Cherokee Dance and Drama

2. The dancing begins and the song is repeated seven times.

3. The leader signals with his rattle, the dancing continues, and one or two women wearing leg-rattles enter the column behind the leader, who holds his rattle at a greater height. The song is repeated four times.

4. The leader holds the rattle aloft, shakes it in tremolo, and the dancers face center, stomping heavily (a'stayi:'disti:yi:', "faster and harder") in one position. At the termination of this high point of the dance the leader rattles in tremolo and the men whoop (a't'ohi:stiyi:', [habitual cry or shout]) or yell, and all break rank.

The gait is the simple, alternating shuffle common to eastern North America, with the knee bent a little and the body relaxed and inclined forward. The dancers keep in close formation one behind the other. The leader may vary the pattern by advancing sideways to the left, and is imitated by the rest of the company. The women move their feet in a shuffle of 3 or 4 inches, with rather more grace than the men. The arms hang limp at the sides except when the men imitate the hand motions of the leader at the turns of the song, by raising the hands to the shoulders or to the head. The only attempts at dramatic gesture are as specified in the appropriate places, and if the Cherokee dance performances are witnessed in the style of the Plains Indian it may be interpreted as recent acculturation from Western sources.

Although feather ornaments and masks are worn, no face painting has been observed among Eastern Cherokee dancers in recent times.

Dances are often held during a week-end period, or Christmas week, or occasionally to welcome a visitor to the Cove. The size of the assembly is affected by weather, seasonal work, the local dance quarters, the prestige of the host, and the like.

# Repertory of Dances

### THE BOOGER OR MASK DANCE

tsu'niɢādu''lĭ, "many persons faces covered over"; <aɢā'dulā'', "mask"

*Equipment.*—Masks representing exaggerated human features are used; ragged European garb, sheets, and bed quilts are worn over the body and shoulders, often over the head, by members of the masked company. (See Pls. I–VI, X, *a*, and fig. 2.) Buckeye wood (*Aesculus octandra*) is usually used in making masks. The coloring matter is prepared as follows: for red, mixed red clay—freely available in the fields—and pokeberries (*Phytolacca decandra*), lighter shades being obtained from a paler-hued clay or bloodroot (*Sanguinaria canadensis*); for black, charcoal made of chestnut or poplar (*Liriodendron tulipifera*) mixed in warm water, also black walnut (*Juglans nigra*) root and sumach (*Rhus typhina*) berries boiled together for about an hour. When dark brown is desired, black walnut or butternut (*Juglans cinerea*) root is boiled; for medium brown, alder (*Alnus rugosa*). Butterfly root (*Aesclepias tuberosa*) gives a yellow paint. Colors are applied with the fingers and palm of hand, not with a brush.

The dimensions of the masks are suited to fit the male face: 10 to 12 inches long and 6 to 8 inches wide. The wall thickness averages ½ inch. The interior hollowing of the block is done with a gouge of steel and a mallet, the block being worked while held between the knees. Exterior carving is done with a chisel and penknife of modern make. The attachment strings are of woodchuck hide or twisted Indian hemp, rags, or store cord.

Examples of Booger Dance masks are the following made by three Big Cove men—Lawyer Calhoun, Deliski Climbing Bear, and West Long:

A red Indian mask, an extraordinary piece by West Long depicting fearful apprehension, evidently the maker's notion of one of the moods of an Indian warrior. Though it is more representative of a warrior in a Scalp Dance, it was also intended to be worn in the Booger Dance. (See Pl. I.)

Figure 2. Gourd Booger Mask

A dark red face representing an Indian, with heavy black eyebrows and black stains beneath the nose.

An Indian face, with rabbit-head skin tacked on forehead with ears in center; teeth carved like a comb. (See Pl. II.)

Face representing a white man, with eyebrows and mustache of heavy black paint; woodchuck fur on forehead and chin.

Face of white man, pale red, with eyebrows, mustache, and goatee of black paint; opossum fur on forehead.

# Repertory of Dances

Face of white man, with eyebrows, mustache, goatee, and head hair of opossum fur; face bordered with band of black paint.

Face of white man, with hair and mustache of opossum fur; heavy streak of pokeberry stain connecting eyebrows.

Face of black man, charcoal color; opossum fur for front hair; eyebrows, mustache, and goatee pure white; nose not negroid. (See Pl. III.)

Face of black man, white opossum hair as above; eyelids and lips stained with pokeberry juice; teeth carved like a comb.

Face of Indian woman, light red; strands of Indian hair depending from sides, tied below with string, Indian hair banged across forehead; red paint on cheeks. (See Pl. IV.)

Gourd mask representing white man, natural color; nose of gourd neck 3½ inches long, turned down, with gray opossum fur fastened around base, representing phallus and pubic hair; patch of brown bearskin on chin for beard, opossum fur on forehead. (See fig. 2.)

Old black gourd mask representing black man; nose section of gourd fastened on, squirrel tail tied on chin and forehead.

Wasp (*Vespa maculata*) nest converted into mask, perhaps a caricature of a diseased white man; interior cleaned out to leave shell, 1½-inch holes cut for eyeholes, mouth the natural exit of nest. (See Pl. X, *a*.)

Pasteboard mask representing white man, eyeholes and mouth cut out and bordered with black paint; nose of pasteboard sewed on; face and eyebrows bordered with rabbit fur.

Gourd mask with feather trimmings. (See Pl. VI.)

John Witthoft has kindly provided us with the following note on the mask-making tradition:[1]

Recent mask-making tradition seems to be restricted to a small segment of the Eastern Cherokee. Will West Long, Lawyer Calhoun, Deliski Climbing Bear, all of Big Cove, made wooden masks as well as those of gourd, wasp

[1] For notes to chapter 2 see page 100.

( 27 )

# Cherokee Dance and Drama

nest, fur, and cardboard in recent years. Eps Welch of Bird Town and his predecessor, Ducksoup, made Booger Dance masks of fur and cardboard. Will's tradition was acquired in his youth from an aged cousin, Charley Lossie, and like the tradition of other Big Cove mask-makers, seems to have been handed down within a select group. Lossie's deer masks are said to have been characterized by attached deer antlers. The only example of a mask which seems to pertain to an earlier period is the specimen illustrated by Olbrechts.[2] This was an heirloom acquired by West Long from another Big Cove family, and old informants agree that this mask was not made by Lossie or later craftsmen but must pertain to a still earlier period in the life of the Big Cove community. Thus the mask-making tradition of the Big Cove appears to be the work of a small group of ritual leaders, and can be traced back far enough to be certain that it is not the result of recent innovation. Allen West Long, the only present-day mask-maker, is West Long's successor.

*Participants.*—A company of four to ten or more masked men, occasionally a couple of women companions (perhaps a phase of a mutual-aid company, gadugi: ), representing "people from far away or across the water"—Germans, French, Chinese, Negroes, or even alien Indians, each wearing an appropriate mask. One legendary notion held that the dancers were to prepare for friendship with strangers, some of whom would have long hair, like a tail, on top of the head. This induced the older Cherokee to identify the Chinese with the prophetic legend, and the masker who wears a long pigtail usually calls himself Chinese. Deliski Climbing Bear in 1929 told Dr. Arthur Kelly that one of the masked party will wear a live sparrow hawk attached as a sign of chieftainship at the Mask Dance.

Each masked dancer has a personal name, usually obscene, which is given upon request to the host of the house party. Maskers pretend to speak other languages than Cherokee, and then only in whispers, to the host; they may cough, clear the throat, and growl. The masks representing Europeans show exaggerations of features—bushy eyebrows, mustaches, chin whiskers, red cheeks, big noses, ghastly white

# Repertory of Dances

pallor, and bald heads. (See Pl. V.) Animal masks are occasionally worn by the Boogers when they desire to represent themselves as hunters and when they carry guns, bows, or clubs. Other equipment of Boogers as hunters may be a dead chicken to represent a wild turkey, a dead lamb, or the skull of a cow or horse. Boogers may distort their figures by stuffing abdomen, buttocks, or shins. Some carry an imitation phallus of gourd neck or wrapped cloth concealed beneath a quilt or sheet, which they expose when dashing toward women and girls. Sometimes the gourd phallus contains water, which is released, adding to the burlesque.

The names given by the maskers or Boogers lend an obscene dramatic element to their individual acts. The following are the names of a company of maskers at one performance in Big Cove on January 2, 1935: German (leader of the maskers), Black (man), Black Buttocks, Frenchman, Big Testicles, Sooty Anus, Rusty Anus, Burster (Penis), Making Pudenda Swell. There is a category of conventional obscene names for the Boogers, although original appellations, when appropriate to the ribald spirit of the performance, are frequent and much applauded. At another dance nationalistic names prevailed, such as Southerner, Northerner, Spaniard, Chinaman. The wearer of a wasp-nest mask was said to represent "hornet," a "mean creature," a character frequently taken by the Boogers.

On one occasion a bear actor, wearing a bear mask, growled and crawled on all fours. He dramatized the tale of a man who was lost and found a she-bear, lived with her, and had offspring. He hibernated with her and she fed him with chestnuts which she produced by rubbing her palms whenever he was hungry. She foretold her death by hunters; finally the hunters came with dogs and she was called out and killed. She had told him to look behind, after she was killed, and he would see her return to life. He did so and saw that she had come back to life. Then the hunters found the bear-man and were glad to get him and took him home. It was a year before the hair dropped off his arms and he became tame. This dramatization of a myth has totemic overtones.

The one or two women masked as females who occasionally form part of the Booger gang are not called upon to give a solo clown dance as are the men. They remain seated on a log or plank bench until the final dance movement in which all the masked actors take part.

In comparative reference we may note that there is no religious symbolism in the contemporaneous function of the Booger Dance among the Eastern Cherokee, and there is no evidence of a masked cult. Unlike Iroquoian practice, the Boogers, or masks, are not initially carved on a living tree to imbue them with life, nor are they referred to as "grandfathers," offered tobacco, fed by being rubbed with grease, kept face upward, or protected from ridicule. But Dr. William N. Fenton has pointed out to us that Cherokee, like Iroquois, masks speak in whispers. No feast is held during the celebration. Olbrechts, however, notes a spiritual association in the taboo against allowing a pregnant woman to look at the masks.[3] According to West Long, in olden times powerful witches existed that could make the unborn child look as horrible as the mask its mother had looked at, but now they are no longer so powerful.

The dance is introduced as a major dramatic and symbolic feature of the night dance series and is not presented as an independent rite. Needless to say, all conversations are in Cherokee.

*Prelude.*—For half an hour or so the members of the house party perform several social dances or one of the usual night series of animal dances. The audience may reach a high stage of excitement. Audible crepitation from women and children is not unusual, although these undisciplined releases are contrary to Cherokee etiquette. On one animated and dramatic occasion, in the log house of Will Pheasant in 1935, a group of about forty persons in taut suspense awaited the entrance of the maskers, and crepitation could readily be

# Repertory of Dances

perceived. When the first invader was questioned about his nationality and identity, he resoundingly broke wind and this was greeted by risible applause. Another of the ten masked performers announced himself with a similar signal. West Long, singer of the occasion, had no explanation for the wind-letting of the Boogers, beyond an observation that it was characteristic of the freedom of the pantomime. Anything might be expected in the excitement and dramatic license prevailing on the night of the Booger Dance.

*First action.*—The masked company, led by a spokesman, boisterously enters the house where the night dance party is being held. The maskers are systematically malignant. On entering, some of them act mad, fall on the floor, hit at the spectators, push the men spectators as though to get at their wives and daughters, and chase the girls toward the crowded walls. The maskers then quiet down and take seats on a board or log bench along the wall. Singing by the musicians of the house party precedes and accompanies the entry.

*Second action.*—The host of the house party announces the arrival of strangers and inquires for the leader of the maskers, who is pointed out by his company. The host then converses in whispers with the leader, asking who the "visitors" are, whence they come, and where they are going. He "interprets" the answers aloud to the house party, who are surprised that they are from a distant land and going "north" or "south." Next the host asks them what they came for and what they want. The response is decisive and candid—"Girls!" (The informant commented with a wag of the head upon the demands of the Boogers: "The Boogers want girls. Oh! they are after them! Chase them around!") There is more surprise and agitation on the part of the host company.

The Boogers may also want "to fight." Both these demands are associated with Europeans, and the Indian house-party leader says they are a peaceable people and do not want to fight. Next the Booger leader says they want to dance, and to this the Cherokee leader agrees. The tonemic pun in the use of the terms here is worth noting. "Fight" is di'ĭsti:, falling accent on the first syllable, while "dance" is diǐsti':, rising accent on the final syllable. The Booger leader, who is not supposed to speak Cherokee too well, thus makes a joke in his "pidgin Cherokee."

The host of the house dance interprets the conclave with the Boogers aloud in Cherokee to the gathering and then adds a few remarks tending to divert the Boogers from their purposes. He announces that the Cherokee would like to know who these strangers are by name. Then he goes to the Booger spokesman and whispers his question. This leads to the following Rabelaisian exhibition.

*Third action.*—The leader of the Boogers whispers his mask name to the host upon request, and the host speaks the name aloud. (See Pl. XII, *a*.) Then the singers of the house party, four to ten in number, the head singer with a drum and the others with rattles, commence the Booger Dance song proper. The name given by the Booger is taken for the first word of the song. The song is repeated four times, while the owner of the name dances a solo in the open space, stamping with both feet, bending body forward, dancing alternately on right and left foot with body canted and the other leg nearly horizontal. He performs awkward and grotesque steps, as if he were a clumsy white man trying to imitate Indian dancing. Each time his name occurs in the song, the whole company applauds and yells. At the conclusion of the song the masker resumes his seat. A similar dance, which lasts about five minutes, is enacted by each Booger (see Pl. XII, *b*) when he has given his name in a whisper and had it loudly announced, until all the masked visitors have competed in drawing applause by their obscene names and clowning.

The maskers do not speak or yell but indulge in exhibitionism, making dashes toward the corner of the house where the women and children are grouped, thrusting their buttocks out and occasionally displaying toward the women large gourd phalli concealed under their clothing.

# Repertory of Dances

After the individual exhibitions of the masked men, the host in a whisper inquires if the maskers would like to dance. The masked spokesman in reply whispers his choice of either the Bear or the Eagle Dance. These are the customary requests, although it is understood that the Pigeon Dance is permissible in this interval. Only one of the selected dances may be performed by the Boogers. An intermission of some five or ten minutes follows the decision on the dance to be given, and in the interval the Boogers may remain within or rush boisterously outdoors for a rest and air. An Eagle rite takes place either before or after the Eagle Dance or Bear Dance, as requested.

*Interlude* (Smoking the Singers and Rewarding the Eagle-Killer).— A sacrifice payment is due to the person who has succeeded in killing the eagle, whose feathers are required in making eagle wands. (See Pl. XV.) The Eagle Dance may take place as the final event in the program of the Boogers. If the Bear Dance is chosen by the Boogers instead of the Eagle Dance, this movement may be omitted. The privilege of killing the eagle is a sacred one, calling for particular recognition in the winter rites.

The singers of the house party at this point continue their chorus with a song in which the word ats"ləgi:ss.ki:', "smokes" (literally, "it's tobacco"), dominates. This is a formal demand for a sacrifice gift for their offices. The Driver then fills and lights a pipe; tradition would prescribe a pipe of stone, made in native style by the Cherokee, but anything will now suffice. He takes one puff himself, facing the fire and with his back to the Boogers. Then he holds the pipe to the mouth of the drummer and each of the singers, giving each a puff. This accomplished, he puts the pipe away. In this smoking rite we discern the pattern of the calumet ceremony so widespread and important in the Eastern Woodlands, the Central Algonkian region, and the Plains.[4] Cognates of the Iroquois ceremonies are found throughout the Eagle Dance ritual.

The Driver has, at a convenient pause during this interval, placed a deerskin on the floor before the Eagle-Killer, upon which he spreads the donation or ceremonial compensation to the dramatic star of the evening, the Eagle-Killer.[5] The donation or sacrifice until recently included a deerskin (for moccasins?), some tobacco (for nerves?), a knife, lead and powder (for livelihood), and buttons and pins (for his womenfolk), while most recently the gift of five cents has superseded payment in kind.

*Fourth action.*—After the interlude of donations and smoking, the singers initiate the requested Eagle (p. 39) or Bear (p. 44) Dance. This is the distinctive dance of the Boogers (see Pls. XIII and XIV) and the maskers perform to the accompaniment of the singers of the house party. A number of women dancers, equaling the number of Boogers, enter the line as partners during the second song of the dance. One woman wears the turtle leg-rattles and assigns herself as partner to the Booger leader. The women are nicely dressed in Cherokee style. Their entry is a symbol of the submission of the Indians to the will of the invader, the gratification of his carnal demands. The erotic display is more overt when the Boogers have called for the Bear Dance than when the Eagle Dance has been chosen. As soon as the women join the dance the Boogers begin their sexual exhibitions. They may close upon the women from the rear, perform body motions in pseudo-intercourse; some protrude large phalli made of gourd necks and these they thrust toward their partners with appropriate gestures and body motions. The women proceed serenely and the Boogers do not insist upon touching them during the dance movement. The dance continues—a Cherokee analogue of Aristophanes' *Lysistrata*—circling around the corn mortar in the center of the room until the song is ended.

The Boogers now crowd noisily through the door to depart on their mysterious mission. But in breaking forth for new adventures, some of these errant gallants dash among the women and clumsily try to drag a struggling victim outside. The women laugh and the girls scream, and off go the Boogers. The Driver may then gather up the gourd rattles and drum from the singers and put them away. (If the rite of Smoking the Singers and Rewarding the Eagle-Killer has not been celebrated before the request dance, it is performed as a finale to the Booger Dance ceremony. At its conclusion the Driver takes the pipe and gives a short circling dance terminating with a cry-command denoting "Stop." He then gathers the rattles and drum and puts them away.)

*Postlude.*—With the disappearance of the maskers the Booger Dance is over and a short recess follows. The house party is now at liberty to continue its night performances without further interruption by the gruesome Boogers, brutish "ghosts" of alien invaders, who, with violent cravings symbolically satiated, have departed in the dark. The leader of the house party resumes his role and the rest of the night is passed in social and animal dances.

It may be worth while to outline the details of a Booger Dance observed during an all-night dance festival in the log house of Will Pheasant at Big Cove on January 7, 1936. There were fifty-three spectators: twenty-three men and boys, sixteen children and infants, fourteen women and girls. In addition there were ten Boogers, all of whom wore white sheets knotted across the chest and below the waist. Most of them entered with arms bound in the sheet and hands folded on groins. One drummer sat on the side and two men with rattles sat on opposite sides of the room. The program was opened with the Beginning Dance. The Boogers entered suddenly, with no announcement, and sat down on a bench between the rattlers. The Driver asked them for their identities and names in succession from right to left. He was told that they came from Germany in search of women and then were going back home. Upon calling their names aloud the Boogers danced singly in succession. Next the Boogers danced together, displaying their grotesque antics. At the termination of this the women joined them, selecting certain Boogers as partners. Then the Boogers went out in the usual boisterous fashion. They removed their masks and quilts in a shed outside and returned to the assemblage, mingling with the audience.

An intermission of about fifteen minutes followed, after which the festival continued with the Women's Dance, atɑho'nɑ (taken from the second movement of the Green Corn Dance rite), the Horse Dance, a repetition of the Beginning Dance, and the Friendship Dance. A random selection of social dances followed, in which the Driver was the master of ceremonies.

In the order of questioning, the names and identities of the Boogers were as follows: a Booger in a black mask (John Driver), a German, tca'mɑni; an unidentified man with a pasteboard mask representing an old white man, Long Phallus, wā"təgɑnɑni:.ta''; Mark Welsh, with bare legs representing another old white man, Sweet Phallus, wātā'u-gɑnast'ā'; an unidentified man wearing a pasteboard mask, Piercer, tigā'ʻk'i:hĩ:'; Steve Watie, wearing a hornet-nest mask, Big Rectum, u'ksəlɛnā''; Gene Driver, wearing a pasteboard mask representing a German with a stuffed hump on his back, Sooty Anus, u'ksᵥtcɔ'ləhi:-tā''; Adam Welch, with a pasteboard mask with brown face, representing a white-robed European, and carrying a gourd phallus, German, tca'mɑni; Henderson Climbing Bear, a sixteen-year-old Booger dressed as a woman with pasteboard mask, wearing pants, with stuffed rags representing a baby carried on the back, carrying a gourd phallus, first gave an inaudible name, then changed it to Her Pudendum Has Long Hairs on It, ulɛstiya' wanāhi:tā'; Nick Driver, wearing a buffalo mask representing a half-human being, Buffalo, yanʻsa''; a half-human creature wearing a bear mask (Ambel Wolf), Bear, yɔnā'.

The term "Booger," equivalent to "bogey" (ghost), is used by English-speaking Cherokee and their white neighbors for any ghost or frightful animal. The actions of the maskers portray the Cherokee estimate of the European invader as awkward, ridiculous, lewd, and menacing, a dramatic perpetuation of the tradition of hostility and disdain. The structure of the Booger Dance is an interesting parallel to the historic masked dramas of the Spanish invasion, staged by the village Indians of Mexico and Central America. It might even be possible to relate the Booger Dance to the expeditions of De Soto, 1540–1542, and Pardo, 1565–1567. The dance may very well possess elements of a mechanism compensatory for national decay and military and cultural defeat.

The dance has the functional value of weakening the harmful powers of alien tribes and races, who, as living beings or ghosts, may be responsible for sickness or misfortune. The Booger Dance may be recommended by a medicine man to form part of a cure for a sick person. The performance would be prescribed in conjunction with and following the procedure of divination by beads and after the family of the afflicted had "gone to the waterside," as required in the cult rite of praying and curing. The process of divination by beads is a simple one; it is used not only for prognosis and diagnosis but in curing disease.

Mooney and Olbrechts[6] define the procedure of "examination with the beads" as follows: "The medicine man holds a black bead between thumb and index finger of the left hand, a white or red bead between forefinger and thumb of the right hand, and, reciting an appropriate formula, examines what are the chances of the sick man. The more vitality the bead in the right hand shows, the greater are the chances for recovery." In diagnosis the same procedure is employed; the medicine man names "a disease causer and asks of the bead whether his statement is right."[7]

It would seem that "examination with the beads" may reveal the agency or dance to be employed for a cure. Should divination disclose the cause of illness to be instigated by Boogers, it would follow that the Booger Dance be the means of relief. Such a prescription may have been the motive for giving the exceptionally dramatic Booger Dance at the home of Will Pheasant on the night of January 2, 1935.

# Cherokee Dance and Drama

As an auxiliary treatment the Booger Dance may be prescribed to "scare away" the spirit causing the sickness. This is an instance where Cherokee masking is associated with medicine in the manner that prevails among the Iroquois. Another use of masks in the practices of curing appears in the following tradition from West Long: "Very long ago the medicine man might employ a mask in conjunction with other means, formulas, and herbs, as a last resort. He would perform his rites before the eyes of the patient, while wearing a mask [type unspecified]. The purpose of this was to excite the patient, as a drastic means of raising the vital quantum. If this measure failed, then the recovery of the sufferer was despaired of."

In its earlier form the Booger Dance, "strong in magic," was undoubtedly limited to winter performance, since its association with "ghosts," those of aliens, is believed to bring killing frosts. Currently, however, it has been observed in all seasons, although it is still performed more frequently in winter.

How did the Cherokee acquire the Booger Dance in the mythical days of Stone Coat? The answer is easy for the Cherokee ceremonialist. Stone Coat revealed to the medicine man a vision of the coming of Caucasians in company with Negroes and strange Indians from the East. He provided the Cherokee with the Booger Dance as a means of counteracting the social and physical contamination which their coming brought upon the natives. The informant's tradition holds that the dance was performed as a protection by the Cherokee sometime before the actual appearance of Europeans. The dance seems to be a combination of dramatic art, protective medicine rite, historical document and prophecy, and moral precept. Lawson, writing in 1714, described a masked clown performance that he witnessed in a Waxhaw village on the Catawba-Wateree River in what is now South Carolina.[8] Although the dance took place several hundred miles east of the Cherokee country, it seems not unlikely that it was a common ceremony in the Carolinas in the eighteenth century.

# Repertory of Dances

Lawson's description is worth quoting, for we can see in it some of the features of the Booger Dance in its present form, the masked antics and the Bear Dance.

Presently in came five men dressed up with feathers, their faces being covered with vizards made of gourds; round their ankles and knees were hung bells of several sorts; having wooden falchions in their hands (such as stage fencers commonly use); in this dress they danced an hour, showing many strange gestures, and brandishing their wooden weapons as if they were going to fight each other; oftentimes walking very nimbly round the room, without making the least noise with their bells, a thing I much admired at; again turning their bodies, arms and legs into such frightful postures that you would have guessed they had been quite raving mad; at last, they cut two or three high capers and left the room. In their stead came in a parcel of women and girls, to the number of thirty-odd, every one taking place according to her degree of stature—the tallest leading the dance and the least of all being placed last; with these they made a circular dance, like a ring representing the shape of the fire they danced about. Many of these had great horse bells around their legs and small hawk bells around their necks. They had musicians, who were two old men, one of whom beat a drum, while the other rattled with a gourd that had corn in it to make a noise withal.[9]

### THE EAGLE DANCE (SYMBOLIC OF VICTORY OR PEACE)

tsuʻgi:daɫi'', "feathers of all kinds," or tətãni'yɛ̃ʻwi:dahĩ:', "they are going to carry solid things," that is, feathers.

*Equipment.*—Eagle-feather wands are made of a rod of sourwood (*Oxydendrum arboreum*) approximately 21 inches long and ½ inch wide, to which is lashed an arch of the same material to serve as a frame for five bald-eagle feathers, about 12 inches long, fastened by inserting the quills through holes in the arch so that they spread out like a fan. (See Pls. XV and XVI.) The sourwood is "sacred" to the eagle rites and prevents contamination when handling the bird and its feathers. Cherokee eagle-feather wands resemble the calumet of the Eastern and Central area both in form and the functions they per-

( 39 )

# Cherokee Dance and Drama

form as emblems of peace. The Cherokee calumet, however, lacks the pipe attachment which distinguished the feathered peace wands of the early historic period.[10]

Each male dancer has a gourd rattle for his left hand, and the leading woman dancer wears tortoise shell leg-rattles in the first and third periods. A singer with a drum is at one side of the group, and there is a fire at one side of the dance plot if the performance takes place at night out of doors.

*Participants.*—An even number of male and female dancers in opposite lines, running east and west, face each other in pairs. The dancers advance a pace, turn, retreat and circle counterclockwise, stop and resume, as described below in the three periods of this rite. Steps range from a dignified walk to the usual shuffling trot, and posture from stooping to crouching with one knee lowered. Undoubtedly it is the most spectacular of Eastern Cherokee dances.

*First period.*—The first period is symbolic of victory. Selected men and women dancers, the men holding feather wands in right hands and gourd rattles in left, the women with wands only, circle around the fire. The feather wands are shaken with quick, short motions up and down, and the gourd rattles are shaken in unison. (See Pl. XV, *a*.) The leading woman dancer wears turtle leg-rattles.

*Second period.*—This takes place early in the night. The dancers circle in crouching postures, jumping around the fire, the men moving clockwise and the women counterclockwise. They stoop, bending one knee nearly to the ground and the other at a right angle (see Pl. XV, *b*), and wave the feather wand up and down, holding it close to the rattle in the other hand. The action is varied by jumping, and a repetition of the motions with wands and rattles.

*Third period.*—This is the Peace-Pipe Dance and occurs toward morning.

*First movement.*—Men and women, in opposed pairs, keep time with the drum by stepping one pace forward and then back to place.

# Repertory of Dances

The dancers alternately pass the feather wands slowly over their partners' heads with lateral, fanlike motions, holding the wands horizontally. (See Pl. XVI, *a*.) At a change of song, the dancers exchange positions and continue waving wands; then they return to the first positions, alternating thus until the end of the song.

*Second movement.*—The dancing pairs continue slowly, waving feather wands over their partners' heads. (See Pl. XVI, *b*.) They advance toward each other and withdraw, over a space of about 10 feet. The opposed dancers then circle halfway, women to the right and men to the left, thus changing the dance partners.

*Third movement.*—The dancers turn, facing outward, and wave the feather wands toward the sky in time with drumming and song. In this movement, which lasts about ten minutes, the men and women approach and separate back to back.

*Concluding movement.*—The dancers face to the right and form in a single column, men together, followed by the women, circling counterclockwise and moving feather wands up and down. The wand is held vertically in the right hand, the rattle in the left, as in the first period. Sometimes the women carry empty baskets, symbolizing the provisions of a feast by the women, to be partaken of by those present at the dance. It is an allegory of feeding the eagle to compensate him for his feathers, and is said to prevent the use of the bird as a medium for working evil and causing sickness by malevolent medicine men.

At the end of the song the leader puts away the wands and the dancers continue with only the rattles. The three stanzas of each song are continued for about ten minutes each, each period of the dance taking about thirty minutes, and the whole over an hour. Any one of the three periods may be enacted independently, as conditioned by time, place, and occasion. The Eagle Dance, it may be noted, is never a regular means of curing sickness among the Cherokee, as it is among the Iroquois. Mooney, however, mentions it as a cure when someone in the settlement has dreamed of eagles or eagle feathers.

# Cherokee Dance and Drama

"He must arrange for an Eagle Dance with the usual vigil and fasting, at first opportunity; otherwise someone of his family will die."[11]

On four occasions when this dance was witnessed, four men and four women took part—a reduction in the traditional number of participants.

Eagle dances were restricted to winter performance because it was believed that if they were celebrated in the spring after frosts had ceased and in summer or fall before the first frosts, they would cause a frost and the destruction of crops. The analogy between enemies, ghosts, and killing frosts lies at the bottom of this restrictive regulation, as it does in the Booger and Bear dances. Mooney[12] associates the rule against summer performance with a fear of having snakes hear the songs of the Eagle Dance, which would make them doubly dangerous. West Long expressed the same belief, adding that in ancient times there were many strong conjurers who sent snakes to carry out their evil intentions.

The Eagle Dance as a peace rite is treated in a short description by Timberlake in the mid-eighteenth century. Comparison of his account with ours shows continuity in the manner of celebrating the peace rites and in the symbolism of the Eagle Dance.

About 100 yards from the town-house we were received by a body of between three and four hundred Indians, ten or twelve of which were entirely naked, except a piece of cloth about their middles, and painted all over in hideous manner, six of them with eagle's tails in their hands, which they shook and flourished as they advanced, danced in a very uncommon figure, singing in concert with some drums of their own make, and those of the late unfortunate Capt. Damere; with several other instruments, uncouth beyond description. Cheulah, the headman of the town, led the procession, painted blood-red, except his face, which was half black, holding an old rusty broad-sword in his right hand, and an eagle's tail in his left. As they approached, Cheulah, singling himself out from the rest, cut two or three capers, as a signal to the other eagle-tails, who instantly followed his example. This violent exercise, accompanied by the band of musick, and a loud yell from the mob, lasted about a minute, when the headman, waving

# Repertory of Dances

## KEY TO DANCE DIAGRAMS
### BASIC FIGURES

 MAN DANCER

 WOMAN DANCER

 SINGER

 DANCER WITH RATTLE

 SINGER WITH DRUM

 MAN WITH GUN

Figure 3

his sword over my head, struck it into the ground, about two inches from my left foot; then directing himself to me, made a short discourse (which my interpreter told me was only to bid me a hearty welcome) and presented me with a string of beads. . . . He had scarce finished, when four of those who had exhibited at the procession made their second appearance, painted in milk-white, their eagle-tails in one hand, and small gourds with beads in them in the other, which they rattled in time to the musick. During this dance the peace-pipe was prepared.[13]

# Cherokee Dance and Drama

Another account is dated half a century later.

The Eagle-tail dance is still in use among the Cherokees. The design of this dance is to stimulate in the minds of the young growing people the spirit of war. The old warriors rehearsing in the dance the dangers they have passed through in attacking their enemies, the distance they have travelled, the time they have been out, &c. Some victuals are usually set apart for the boys to eat at day break, and when the boys have eaten they go out of the town house and are met in the entry by the young men, who have a battle with mud collected for the purpose.

It is also customary to give Eagle feathers as pledges of friendship in making peace among red people.[14]

An omen of interest is associated with the dance. Should one of the dancers carrying the feather wands stumble and fall or even drop his wand, it would mean his death very soon through the conjuring power of a malevolent medicine man. Traditionally, the feather wand must never touch the ground. The loss of compulsiveness of such traditions is indicated by a performance of the Eagle Dance in 1940 at the tourist village trading center. There was much stumbling and the wands were permitted to touch the ground. The air of bravado in this performance suggested that the taboo was known and deliberately violated.

### THE BEAR DANCE

yɔnɑ' dɑdɑ'ɨski:sǐ:', "bear dance"

The dancers circle counterclockwise around the mortar in the center of the room or, if outdoors, around a fire. At one side of the circle is a singer with a drum, who may be aided by another with a gourd rattle.

*First movement.*—The men shuffle and sway their bodies, imitating the leader, who growls like a bear. The dancers respond with grunting when the leader raises the tone of the song and shakes the rattle in tremolo.

# Repertory of Dances

*Second movement.*—The women enter the line ahead of the men as partners, face partners and dance backward several turns, then reverse. The men put their hands on the women's shoulders.

The representation of the dancers as bears, potentially as mates, has of course a certain sexual significance. At one point in the dance the actors raise their heads and tear the air over their shoulders in imitation of the dance presumed to be performed by bears. It is believed that old bears have a dance in which they circle around a big hemlock tree, leaving tooth marks on the bark at head height. West Long himself saw such a marked Bear-Dance tree when he was a boy.

The Bear Dance, which is symbolic of the bear hunt, may be given as an independent performance, but it is usually a major unit in a larger series of dances, such as in the winter ceremonial drama of the Booger Dance.

## SUMMER DANCES

### GREEN CORN CEREMONY AND DANCE

Legend relates that a branch of the Cherokee tribe compressed their infants' heads laterally. The method was for the mother to warm her hands and press on the child's temples every day until it was grown. For this reason the people of this group were called ɒi:ni:kɔhɛ̃nã‘, "big foreheads projecting out people." Like the rest of the Cherokee they had a Green Corn Dance, but they were given to performing it with great devotion at the harvest. So the other Cherokee came to refer to the dance by the name of this group, whence akɔhãdí:‘, Green Corn Dance (literally, "big foreheads in motion").

The dance, which lasts all day and the following night, has four periods. The men's and women's parts are performed separately but concurrently. The dances are sponsored by some person who wishes to make a ceremonial donation from which he gains prestige and spiritual benefit, as do the participants.

( 45 )

GREEN CORN CEREMONY and DANCE

FIRST STAGE
MEN'S PART
FIRST MOVEMENT

DANCE CIRCLE

SECOND MOVEMENT

MAIN DANCE GROUND

Figure 4

# Repertory of Dances

*First stage: Men's part* (uli''sĭ).—The leader is followed by a column of men[16] (ten, twelve, sixteen, or twenty) carrying guns. They circle counterclockwise at the dance station, which is several hundred yards from the main dance ground and feasting place.

*First movement* (see Pl. XVII, *a,* and fig. 4).—The company of selected men dancers circle counterclockwise behind the leader, who sings to the accompaniment of a gourd rattle. Guns are discharged at intervals throughout the morning, beginning with the man at the head of the column, followed by a shot from the next, and so on to the end man, who fires twice. The shots are given at signals in the leader's song and at a rapid shaking of the rattle. The reports from the guns symbolize thunder.

*Second movement* (see fig. 4).—The men dance two abreast, starting from the remote dance station and moving to the main dance ground, with the leader at the head. At the signal asi:hu'yakã they turn suddenly and go back across the space to where they started. This movement takes place about noon, and the men rest from dancing for half an hour to eat food provided by the women of the settlement. There are no food restrictions.

That the use of an explosion is a modern innovation to the rite is denied by the informant, who explained it as follows. Formerly a medicine man was called upon to exercise his magic power to produce a report to accentuate the intervals of the song and dance. As the men danced around, he would sit beside a "big white rock," put charcoal on the rock, spit on the charcoal, and, at the words hi':ha':hi':, strike it with a club (stone). An explosion with a sharp report would result. Later, by the end of the seventeenth century, when the white traders had supplied European arms to the Cherokee, "they substituted guns" for the chemicals. This is a rather interesting example of rationalization in technology. A similar vulcanic feat was reported in 1934 by Deskaheh, a Cayuga ceremonial informant.

*Women's Dance part* (atαhónã'', literally, "make wood," Women's

# GREEN CORN CEREMONY and DANCE
## WOMEN'S PART
## FIRST and THIRD MOVEMENTS

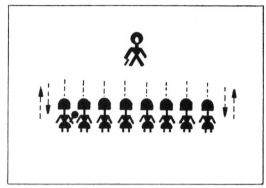

MAIN DANCE GROUND

SECOND MOVEMENT

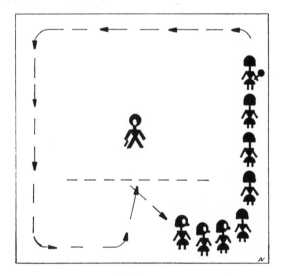

Figure 5

(48)

# Repertory of Dances

Dance or Meal Dance; i:'ł:tsã, literally, "meal," Women's Dance song).—The women dancers (volunteers) gather in the center of the main dance ground at some distance from the men dancers. They are lined up side by side before the main singer and shuffle with short steps. They are accompanied by a man[16] at some distance with a drum and the woman leader, who uses tortoise shell leg-rattles. The Women's Dance may be detached from its ritual context and performed in other dance series such as the Booger Dance.

*First movement* (see fig. 5).—The dancers advance a few feet toward the singer, then retreat. The first part of the movement is in slow time. The last part is accelerated and the file turns right about, advancing and retreating to the singer.

*Second movement* (see fig. 5).—The women follow their leader, who is wearing turtle leg-rattles, circling counterclockwise once around the dance ground. The stanzas of the women's song elicit formal responses from the leader of the men's song group.

*Third movement* (see fig. 5).—The women resume formation abreast, as in the first movement, all holding hands. The woman wearing turtle leg-rattles dances at the left of the row of dancers.

*Combined part.*—At the conclusion of the separate dances for men and women the following takes place.

*First movement* (see Pl. XVII, *b*, and fig. 6).—Starting from the separate dance ground, the men dancers with guns are led by the leader with a rattle in a shuffling trot, two abreast, to the main dance ground. First they surround the women dancers in a large circle, dancing clockwise, then close in tightly around the women's dance line until they merge with it. This repeats the action of the second movement of the men's part.

*Second movement* (see fig. 7).—Men dancers combine with the women's dance column led by the men's dance leader, and mingle with the women, circling counterclockwise.

*Third movement* (see fig. 7).—The man drumming and singing for

( 49 )

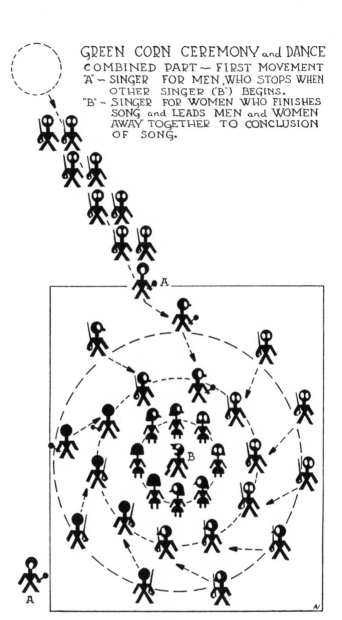

GREEN CORN CEREMONY and DANCE
COMBINED PART — FIRST MOVEMENT
"A" — SINGER FOR MEN, WHO STOPS WHEN
        OTHER SINGER ("B") BEGINS.
"B" — SINGER FOR WOMEN WHO FINISHES
        SONG and LEADS MEN and WOMEN
        AWAY TOGETHER TO CONCLUSION
        OF SONG.

Figure 6

# GREEN CORN CEREMONY and DANCE
## COMBINED PART — SECOND MOVEMENT
### "A" REPLACES "B" IN THIRD MOVEMENT.

Figure 7

the women's party resigns his station to the men's leader with the gourd rattle, who then takes both parties through to the finish, as in the second movement of the women's part.

Although the symbolic value of these movements is not clear, there is implied a fertilization of vital elements, specifically the grains. A short notice of the Green Corn Dance was given by Chief Hicks in 1818.[17]

The green corn dance, so called, has been highly esteemed formerly. This is held when the corn is getting hard and lasts four days, and when the national council sits—a quantity of venison being procured to supply the dance. It is said that a person was formerly chosen to speak to the people on each day in a language that is partly lost—at least there is very little of it known now. At such times as the above, a piece of land is laid off and persons appointed to occupy it—no others being allowed to use it while the feast continues.

*Second stage: feasting interval.*—At the conclusion of the first stage of dancing the entire gathering partakes of the feast provided by the women of the home settlement. "Everyone is invited to share," both strangers and people from other Cherokee towns.

*Third stage.*—This is timed to take place just before sundown. The men and women dancers begin dancing in separate groups as in the first stage. The man singing for the women dancers uses a gourd rattle, but no drum is heard at this time. The women's dance leader wears tortoise shell leg-rattles.

*First movement.*—The men's leader conducts the dancers, who carry guns on their shoulders,[18] toward the women's dance circle, as in the third movement of the combined part. They surround the women and, moving clockwise, close in about them.

*Second movement* (ganã'ni:`, "along the path or trail").—The men dancers mingle with the women dancers, circling counterclockwise and zigzagging, and the men's leader resigns leadership to the women's male leader and singer. This movement continues for about half an hour, until the sun has set.

*Fourth stage.*—The night following the feast is spent in dances chosen from the series of animal rites, with the exception of the Booger, Bear, and Eagle dances. The dances begin with the Friendship Dance and end just before dawn with the Round or Running Dance, which is preceded by the Corn Dance, an intrinsic part of the harvest ceremony. Mooney's informants related that in old times every fire in the settlement was extinguished just before the Green Corn Dance and all the people came and got new fire from the town house.[19]

The performance of the corn rite in the morning has symbolic significance, according to West Long. It represents "early spring planting" through the analogy of morning and the springtime of the year. It is also believed to have been a necessary preparation for planting; the medicine man had an important part to play in offering prayer so that the corn would grow fast. Another purpose of the rite was to prevent the illness believed to result from eating green corn. Like all the tribes of the Southeast, the Cherokee feared the consequences of eating corn before the performance of placatory rites. The drinking of certain medicines in the form of an infusion is also remembered. Though the full particulars of the older Cherokee ceremony are not now known, this portion has been described by Witthoft.[20] From his material it appears that the festival was a major community rite celebrated in August, when the green corn first became mature enough to eat, that it persisted as late as 1887, and that aspects of it are found as two separate survivals, the green corn feast and a green corn medicine. The latter is prepared and administered in the separate households of the conservatives as a prerequisite to eating green corn. West Long did not identify specimens of *Ilex cassine,* source of the "black drink" used on similar occasions by the Creeks and Yuchi, as the ingredient called for in the Cherokee prophylaxis; but the details of the rite might be clarified if they were supplemented by information culled from the narratives of such eighteenth-century travelers as Timberlake, Brickel, and Adair. *Ilex cassine* does not grow in the region now occupied by the eastern Cherokee.

# Cherokee Dance and Drama

A Moravian account of a Green Corn Dance in August, 1803, is given by Schwarze:[21]

While awaiting the session of the Council at Oostanaula, lodged with Standing Turkey near the Town House, the Brethren had opportunity to observe some of the Cherokee dances. They saw five different varieties of Indian dances, all very simple, but some distinguished by great regularity. Each dance was accompanied by the song of two men who also beat time with calabashes filled with small stones. Their principal dance was the "Green Corn Dance," really intended to be a religious exercise of Thanksgiving to "the Man above," for the new crop of corn. Men and women were decked out in their best for these dances, at which good order prevailed. The dancing ground was in front of the Town House, a large, level place swept clean. In the center stood a high pole with green boughs tied to it to afford some shade. At the pole stood a bench upon which were seated those who beat time. One dance is carried out by two groups of men who appear out of the bushes on opposite sides of the dancing ground with loud shouts and advance towards the pole in the center around which they dance in opposite directions. Another dance is done by one group of men who are led by their singer. They carry guns and after they march a little distance to calabash time, the singer quickly turns and bows down to the earth. The whole group then sing with him and likewise bow to the ground and begin to dance around the singer; next, the guns are fired and then they begin all over again! A third dance, in which men and women assist, is carried out in a slow movement around the pole. The singers dance in front and somewhat to one side of the ring, looking very serious and solemn. Another dance employs about sixty Indians who start dancing at the pole and then widen the circle more and more with an interwoven, spiral movement until they reach the limits of the ground, then closing up to the pole again. The last dance the missionaries witnessed was done by women only, dancing around the pole, the men beating time. The female leader of this dance wore leather shoes with turtle backs fastened thereto with which she mightily rattled!

I. Booger Mask by West Long. "Agonized Indian"

II. Booger Mask. Indian Face

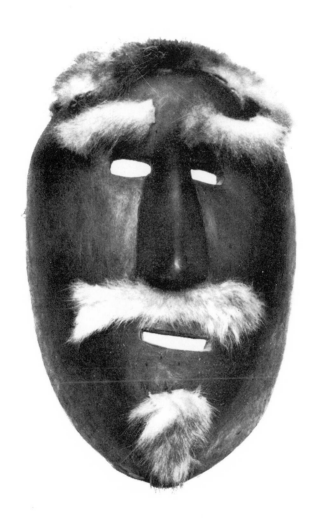

III. Booger Mask. Black Man

IV. Booger Mask. Indian Woman

V. Booger Mask. White Man

VI. Booger Mask. Gourd with Feather Trimmings

VII. Warrior's Mask

VIII. Wildcat Mask. Used in Stalking Wild Turkeys

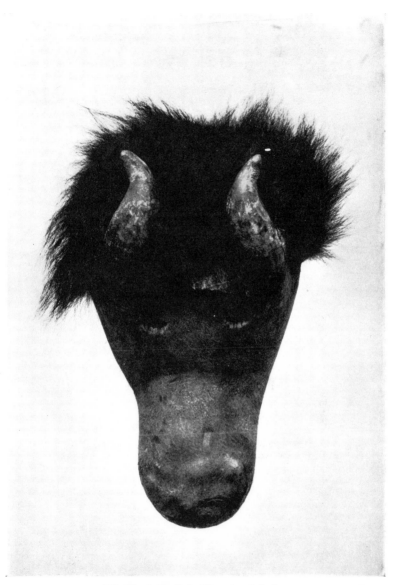

IX. Black Buffalo Hunting Mask

X, *a.*
Booger Mask. Hornet

X, *b.*
Bear-Dance Masker in Dance
Attitude. Corn Mortar and Pestle
in Background

XI, *a*.
Tortoise Shell Leg-Rattles

XI, *b*.
Gourd and Box Turtle
Hand-Rattles Used by
Medicine Men

XII, *a*. The Leader of the Boogers Whispers His Mask Name

XII, *b*. Booger Dance. Solo in the Third Action

XIII, *a*. Booger Dance. Fourth Action

XIII, *b*. Booger Dance. Fourth Action

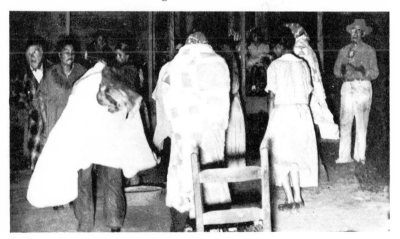

XIV. Booger Dance

XV, *a.*
Eagle Dance. First Period

XV, *b.*
Eagle Dance.
Second Period

XVI, *a.*
Peace-Pipe Dance of the
Eagle Dance

XVI, *b.* Eagle Dance. Third Period, Second Movement

XVII, *a*. Green Corn Dance. First Stage, Men's Part

XVII, *b*. Green Corn Dance. First Stage, Combined Part

XVIII. Ballplayers' Dance

XIX, *a*. Round or Running Dance. Women Circling

XIX, *b*. Round or Running Dance. Serpentine Movement

XX. Friendship Dance

XXI, *a*. Pigeon Dance

XXI, *b*. Partridge Dance

## XXII
## Lawyer Calhoun

# Repertory of Dances

## BALLPLAYERS' DANCE

dã`tsɛlã` nũni:'', "things transformed"; dɑnɛ`ksi:nɑtani:'', "they are going to put the things on their buttocks"

*Equipment.*—The pairs of sticks used in the Ball Game are also used here. Formerly, a "tail" pendant, usually made of feathers, was suspended from the rear of a belt. Such ornaments were symbolic of speed and strength, and were appropriate to the Ball Game rather than the dance. The tails were made of feathers of hawk, white goose, or eagle, or occasionally of a deer's tail.

The bone scratchers used to scarify the arms, backs, and chests of the ballplayers are of considerable importance in the ceremonies throughout the Southeast; their manufacture and use are restricted to medicine men. Their purpose is to purify and strengthen the subject in anticipation of the dangers and struggles of the Ball Game, and in former times as preparation for war. The following are examples of instruments used in scarifying dancers and players.

A single fang from the upper jaw of a banded rattlesnake (*Crotalus horridus*) attached to the quill of a white duck feather by splitting the quill and binding it with white thread. The feather symbolizes speed of flight, and a strand of red thread tied to the middle of the quill symbolizes lightning and its destructive speed and force. (This was obtained from Deliski Climbing Bear, who owned its secret and the right to manufacture it. Olbrechts was unable to obtain a specimen of the rattlesnake scratcher at the time of his investigation.)

A wild turkey quill trimmed to within 3 inches of the tip was bent to form a rectangular frame, 1 by 2 inches, for seven sharpened slivers of turkey-wing bone. The slivers were evenly spaced within the opening so that the sharp points projected slightly below the edge. The ties and lashings were of Indian hemp.

A similar turkey-bone scratcher lacked the quill projection and used white thread as well as Indian hemp. The specific symbolic values are

# BALLPLAYERS' DANCE
## MEN'S PART

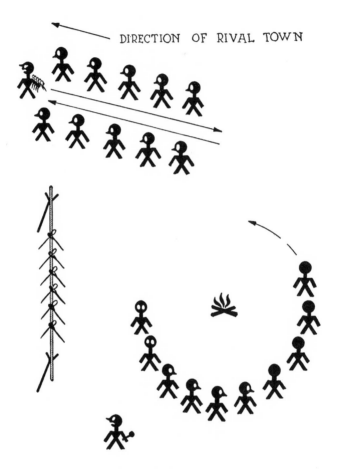

DIRECTION OF RIVAL TOWN

Figure 8

# Repertory of Dances

as follows: deer tail represents swiftness; white goose-feather "tail," or one worn in the hair, distinguishes the swiftest player; the eagle or hawk, preferably falcon, feather represents the strongest player. The ballplayers themselves choose the kind of "tail" they would wear, making their selection to represent their chief skill. A claim when established and denoted by the emblem of the "tail" would not be challenged by others, but a false claim would elicit ridicule and disgrace. Ballplayers sometimes wore headbands of ground-hog skin, with feathers and decorations of the same symbolic value as the pendants.

The usual number of teeth in the scratchers is five or seven, and the quill may be from a large hawk or falcon, as well as the wild turkey. West Long indicated that the leaves of the fetterbush or dog hobble (*Leucothoë catesbaei*) were also used as scratchers. The scratcher made of laurel leaves noted by Dr. Olbrechts could not have been identified correctly, since the leaf ends are too tender to penetrate the skin.

The medicine man who acts as singer uses a gourd rattle, the neck of which serves as a handle. The rattle may be decorated with an eagle or a hawk-feather pendant to signify speed and strength for the players. The leader of the women dancers may wear leg-rattles when the rite is performed by the Bird Town band, but at Big Cove this is not customary. The drum is used by the singer in parts of the women's dances.

The dance is performed outdoors in a secluded place, often on an island or near the bank of a stream to enable the performers to "go to water." Here they camp on the night before the game. The dance may be repeated near the goal posts before starting the game.[22]

*Men's part* (see fig. 8).—There may be ten to fourteen ballplayers, who are augmented by other men who are willing to take the preliminary preparations if they are to be selected to play. All are supposed to submit to the tests imposed by the conjurer who conducts

( 57 )

# Cherokee Dance and Drama

the rites, and the best are chosen to play the next day. Between the dances, seven specially selected men go to the stream bank where the conjurer is concealed and attend him while he prays to strengthen them and weaken their opponents. The dancers carry their ball sticks and at the end of each dance the Driver collects the sticks from the dancers, carrying them hooked in pairs over each arm, the handle of one stick run through the loop of the other, forming an inverted **V**. He takes them to a horizontal pole supported on crotched uprights and suspends them in a row. The pole is located on the side of the fire nearest the settlements of the rival team. If the number of intended players is large it may require two attendants to carry the ball sticks back and forth between the pole and the dancers during the dance intervals.

*Regular movement.*—The dancers circle counterclockwise around the fire with shuffling steps. The singer is at the left of the ring with a rattle. Dances are called at intervals by the Driver, who instructs players to prepare for the dance, then takes the ball sticks from the rack and hands a pair to each dancer. One of the dancers gives a whoop of defiance at the rival settlement and the others answer him with supporting yells.

There are four principal songs for the men's dances, and at the end of each song and dance the men's conjurer or singer gives the signal ho:kwā:`, "halt." Then he defies the rival players and conjurer, and "teases" them in order to weaken them. At Bird Town the procedure varies somewhat: several players charge in the direction of the opponents' settlement, brandishing ball sticks like weapons and whooping defiance.

*Alternate movement* (see fig. 8).—Seven times during the night performance, at intervals of about an hour, the conjurer arranges the players and candidates in parallel rows facing the "enemy's" town. The conjurer selects a man who is a good whooper, whether or not he is a player, to symbolize an attack on the "enemy." The actor runs

# Repertory of Dances

between the rows of players toward the rival town, carrying ball sticks across his left arm. He stops about ten paces beyond the columns and shouts formal cries of defiance; seven times he cries gᾱ, and ends with a whoop, striking his lips to make a tremolo. He turns, runs back between the lines, ending with a jump, and shouts dedu'ni:ɛɫᾱ', signifying "weak, unsuccessful, to no purpose." The office is called talā'la' and represents the redheaded woodpecker (*Melanerpes erythrocephalus*),[28] a bird possessing attributes of power of beak and flight. The players and candidates then start at once to dance again, the resumption song being the weyu'haha'. Strong Plains parallels may be noted in this part of the sequence.

One of the songs chanted for the men in their dance contains the repeated refrain hɛn.lo hi: sᾱ, equivalent to "least flycatcher (*Empidonax minimus?*), look!" This has reference to the speed and accuracy of the eye of this bird, which can seize an insect in flight. An alternating stanza of the song ends with hi:yᾱ in place of hi:sᾱ—hi:yᾱ being an imitation of the cry of the bird. During this chant the dancers go through motions of catching and throwing the ball.

The proximity of the dancers to the smoke of the fire may have some connection with the idea of purification, of common occurrence in eastern North America. At least during the performance of the last dance before morning a heavy smoke produced by a quantity of pine wood thrown on the fire was intended to increase their strength.

At the conclusion of each repetition of this movement the dancers go to a secluded place at the stream near by, where the conjurer is waiting for them to perform his magical ministrations in which he prays to strengthen them and weaken their enemies. A pregame ceremony was observed in 1935 at which only the ball sticks were immersed in the stream, and on occasion the participants in this phase of the water rite may permit water to drip from the sticks into their mouths.

At each interval, as soon as the men dancers have left the fire around which they dance to "go to water" where the medicine man is waiting for them, the women dancers take up. They are accompanied by their medicine-man singer and leader with the drum.

*Women's part* (see Pl. XVIII and fig. 9).—Seven women, who aboriginally may have represented the seven clans, take part in these dances. Although those chosen are expected to continue their performance all night, other women may at times join in if they wish. Like the male dancers, the women face the opponents' town to work their spell against it. The figure of speech applying to their dance action is that they are "stepping on the players of the opposite town."

In some of the dance songs, for instance when singing yahowi yukane, they chant with the male singer; in others they dance silently while the conjurer sings. The women's dance singers are conjurers called upon by the Driver, and each takes a turn. There may be as many as ten songs in the women's series.

The women begin their dances standing abreast in a line a few paces from the fire on the side nearest to the rival settlement and just behind the rack supporting the ball sticks. Toward the end of their dances they circle the fire, and when the players return the women cease dancing.

The final dance of the women's series, which takes place just before morning, is a quickstep around the fire. At its conclusion they too are "taken to water," following their conjurer as the players have previously done. At the water's edge they wash their faces and hands. On the way "to the water" their singer starts the least flycatcher song, and while this is sung the women imitate ball-playing, as did the men when the song was chanted for them.

The Ball Game or Ballplayers' Dance is but a small part of a long, involved, and esoteric ritual preparation for the team, to add spiritual strength to its efforts and to weaken those of its opponents. Its analogies are martial and the entire performance corresponds with ancient rites of the war party. The gaming feature need not be regarded as a

# BALLPLAYERS' DANCE
## WOMEN'S PART

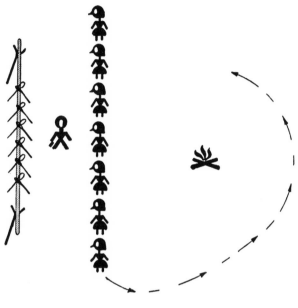

Figure 9

step toward profanation, for it is associated with rites throughout eastern North America in the Iroquois Bowl Game, Lacrosse, and the Tug of War, as well as the widespread Moccasin Game.

The ballplayers who finally have been selected by the medicine man are subjected to the scratching ordeal and purification just before the game. For a description of the scratching operation see Mooney and Olbrechts.[21]

During the preparation three longitudinal, parallel scratches were made upon the upper arms, lower arms, upper legs, and lower legs of the players. A half circle, opening downward, was made upon the chest and back. Sometimes the medicine man used a splinter of glass to let blood, taking in all almost half a pint, it is said. If the blood ran dark he drew more until it ran light red, although no explanation is available for this procedure. Kaloski (Standing Deer), an old-time ball-play expert, asserted that the scratching was inflicted to make the players avoid being seized by their opponents. The players were urged to chew slippery elm and spit it upon their bodies, to make them more slippery when sweating. A good-luck symbol, in the form of a cross or a semicircle with dot, may be marked with charcoal from the dance fire on the cheeks, foreheads, chests, or backs of the players.

## War Rites

### WAR OR SNAKE-MASK DANCE

i:nɑDā'i:yu'stī'', "snakelike"

*Equipment.*—Wooden mask with coiled rattlesnake carved on forehead or crown (see Pl. VII), gourd rattle of medicine type, and one or two sets of turtle leg-rattles. One example of a mask used was medium red, representing an Indian; the eyeholes were bordered with black, gray fox fur was on the top and sides of the head, and a coiled rattlesnake, the rattles inside the coils, was carved in high relief on the forehead; teeth were carved in the mouth. Another Indian-face mask had a snake carved on the black crown, with rattles showing plainly; woodchuck fur was on the head, and no teeth were represented. In an interview with Dr. Arthur Kelly in 1929, Climbing Bear said that the chief of the dance party customarily attached a live sparrow hawk to the snake mask. West Long was unable to confirm this information.

*First movement.*—A warrior wearing a snake mask dances counterclockwise around the fire with a slow march step. Behind him is the singer, followed in turn by a woman with turtle leg-rattles, and other warriors.

*Second movement.*—The warrior takes a position behind the woman with leg-rattles. The singer leads the file and carries the song burden while the others sing an accompaniment.

The dance dramatizes the warrior's defiance of human enemies, of witches and ghosts, "to show lack of fear of anything" by wearing a mask in the image of a rattlesnake. Aboriginally, it was probably an enlistment dance, a challenge to others to join in a war party. Deliski Climbing Bear said that the serpent masks have no specific ceremonial value. Rather, they indicated to the other dancers that the men wearing them were soon going on the warpath against, let us say, the Catawba, the Seneca, or the English.

### WARRIOR OR BRAVE DANCE

*Equipment.*—Ceremonial war clubs colored red (symbolizing blood, "enemy hit on head") and black (symbolizing anger, "not afraid of anything"). There is a singer with a drum at one side of the platoon of warriors.

*First movement.*—The warriors stand abreast in a line facing east, with clubs in their right hands. Leaning forward they dance with a slow, low step forward and backward. At the signal he ha li, the dancers emit a prolonged war cry, <ye> <ye>.

*Second movement.*—The song changes to quick time and the dancers make motions to strike the enemy with their clubs.

*Third movement.*—The dancers mill about with a quickstep and conclude with four whoops.

The dance represents an advance against the enemy and anticipated combat. The last serious and dramatic performance of which there is record was in the time of Junaluska, a noted chief who fought the Creeks in support of General Jackson (1813–1814), and died in 1858.[25] The Warrior Dance has become a traditional stereotype. It is understood that originally the warriors underwent strenuous rites for the strengthening of their powers, physical and spiritual. We are told that for a class of consecrated warriors no weapon other than the club

# Cherokee Dance and Drama

was needed in conflict; the magic power of the club alone, when strengthened by the medicine man's rites, was sufficient. The original clubs were of heavy oak or hickory; the ceremonial clubs now prepared for the dance are of buckeye (*Aesculus octandra*).

### VICTORY OR SCALP DANCE (PART OF EAGLE DANCE)

*First movement.*—A line of warriors, each with a feather wand in his right hand and in wartime a scalp in his left, circles around the dance space. A singer carrying a drum is near the center of the line, and the warriors give intermittent whoops.

*Second movement.*—The song ceases and the dancers walk slowly behind the warrior at the head of the line while he recites and acts out a brief account of his exploits. The dance leader then takes his feather wand and gives place to the next warrior.

*Third movement.*—The Victory Dance song is resumed with the second warrior at the head of the line, carrying the feather wand and the scalp.

*Fourth movement.*—The warrior at the head of the line recites; then, relinquishing the feather wand to the leader, goes behind, leaving the next man at the head.

The movements are repeated until all the warriors have been conducted around the circle and have taken a turn at reciting their exploits. Much whooping and sustained yelling takes place at the beginning and end of songs and recitations. The drumming is interrupted during the recitation of exploits. At the conclusion of the dance the feather wands (and formerly the scalps) are collected and put away by the leader.

The dance is a historical pageant and boasting pantomime of warriors' exploits. The eagle-feather wands are a symbol of victory and courage. The rite is analogous to counting "coup" of the Plains area. Needless to say, it has been a mere form in the Cherokee dance program for more than a century.

# Repertory of Dances

## FORMAL RITES

### BEGINNING DANCE

yεłułɛ'', "standing in center," refers to dancers standing gathered in front of the door, then entering house behind leader when he has started a few bars of the first song.

*Equipment.*—The dance leader carries a gourd rattle; one or two women behind the leader wear turtle shell leg-rattles. On one occasion, in January, 1935, there were two singers leading, one using a gourd rattle and the other carrying a drum.

*First movement.*—The dancers, forming a single file with the sexes alternating, circle counterclockwise and then advance.

*Second movement.*—The men face the women and dance backward once around, then swing partners; the women dance backward, reverse, and resume the first position. During this movement the men engage in acts of innocent familiarity with the women partners who have joined the file; the men sometimes hold the women's hands, clasp them palm to palm, or place them on their shoulders.

The dance, which resembles the Friendship Dance, opens the series of annual rites or social dances and is formally a social introduction. It dramatizes hospitality and familiarity through association first as neighbors in a dance and then as partners.

### FRIENDSHIP DANCE

di:łsti':, "mixed," refers to changing of song theme by different leaders.

*Equipment.*—Only tortoise shell leg-rattles worn by the woman following the leader are used.

*Movement.*—The men form a single file and are joined by women who dance in front of them as partners. During the song they dance counterclockwise with a shuffling trot, and in the intervals walk in a

( 65 )

# Cherokee Dance and Drama

circle. At the second song in the series, when the leader begins to insert words suggestive of intimacy (see translations below), the humorous gestures and acts of the pantomime begin. (See Pl. XX.) The sequence of intimacy is as follows: (*a*) partners are greeted by holding hands during that portion of the song when they dance facing; (*b*) the partners dance side by side, holding hands crossed; (*c*) dance facing, putting palms upon partners' palms; (*d*) place hands on their partners' shoulders while dancing facing; (*e*) place arms over partners' shoulders while dancing side by side; (*f*) place hats on women partners' heads while dancing facing; (*g*) stroke partners under chin while dancing facing; (*h*) put hands on female partners' breasts while dancing side by side; (*i*) touch the clothing over the partners' genitals while dancing side by side. During the last two phases the file crowds together, partially to conceal familiarities. These phases are usually omitted when whites are spectators.

During the song the leader may raise his hands, palms in, to shoulder height, at times turning halfway to the left and moving sideways. He is imitated by the men dancers, who then dance backward facing their partners. At the conclusion of the song the dancers hold hands; at the change of song they zigzag while circling; at next change they reverse direction.

Patently, this is a social pantomime of the course of intimacy between the sexes, beginning with acquaintance made at the dance and developing through various stages of familiarity into the intimacy of courtship and sexual intercourse.

The words are sung by the various leaders selected by the Driver; choral responses are made by the assistant leader and male dancers. West Long chose the texts recorded as typical of the performance.

hā hā         (An exclamation of welcome surprise at the woman partner who steps in line behind him; it is given in a teasing fashion.)

# Repertory of Dances

| | |
|---|---|
| agɛ'hyã | woman |
| o'hi | good |
| ha'ni: | here |
| ɛhe''i: | living |
| | (Connotation: I did not know there was such a good shell rattle-shaker living.) |
| akayã'li: | old fellow |
| hanɔ'se | that's what [they] call him |
| ikk:ɑ'yi: | he is in front [leading] |
| a:lɛ'hu | he is standing while in motion |
| awi:'nɑ | young man |
| i:yu'sti: | looks like |

The song is interrupted with whoops while the dance continues.

| | |
|---|---|
| kayu'wadu'hi | pretty woman |
| tə ga:'tinhɛ'si | I am going to take home with me |
| kani:'ki:tã' | none |
| agɛ'hyã | woman |
| ti:ki:tuhũ'i: | where is my town? [settlement] |

A free rendering is as follows: "I am called an old man [poor and ugly] but I am not this. I am going to take this woman home with me, as I did not know that there was such a good shell-shaker, none like her. I'll take her home to my settlement."

Toward the end of the selection when this text was recorded, the leader reaches the climax of his humor in the following phrase, di:'ta sɑn'hɛ hĩ:', "we are going to touch each other's privates"; the men, holding their partners' hands, suit actions to words. If the woman is a relative in any degree, however, they simply continue to hold hands.

The same or another leader may resume the dance with a similar song. Some are variations of the form just given and others are freer compositions, depending on the ability and experience of the leaders.

# Cherokee Dance and Drama

The following are devoid of erotic suggestion.

| | |
|---|---|
| hi:yatsitu' hi:hi:'yo | (No word meaning) |
| tuya:ˋtət'ᾱ' | something has branches at the top (meaning the Oklahoma country, by some analogy which is not clear) |
| ti:yɔhi:t.la'' | land lizard |
| huni:kɔhɛ' | they saw |
| ɛ:kwɔhi:' | big |
| i:kit'ᾱ | size |
| atsi:lahā' | all afire |
| diti:'k'a'nhɛ' | he was looking at us |
| nᾱ' yahā' | all rocks (meaning the Rocky Mountains) |
| ɔtali'' | over the big mountains |

The verse depicts the country of the Western Cherokee nation and has great sentimental value for the Eastern band.

### ROUND OR RUNNING DANCE

atɛ'hyɔ̃hĩ:', "around habitually"

In this dance the women start circling counterclockwise in a slow step through four slow songs. They are led by a woman wearing leg-rattles, and the singer with a drum is at one side. (See Pl. XIX, *a*.) When the song changes to quick time the men join in, coming between the women as their partners, a reversal of the usual order of acquiring partners. A serpentine movement may occur here as a variant of the circular. (See Pl. XIX, *b*.) The songs are terminated by shouts. No mimicry takes place, and there are no motions or symbols. It is the final dance of the night series and ceases with the dawn.

Being a concluding dance, the Round Dance usually includes all the members of the dance group. Often there are two groups of dancers circling side by side.

# Repertory of Dances

### BEAVER DANCE

ᴅəyi′′ ᴅɑnɑˋtsˋki:′sĩ′, "beaver they dance"; also ᴅəni:′ɑ̃hi:li:ˋ, "going to hit lightly with something," which has reference to the striking of the beaver effigy in the second movement.

*Equipment.*—Each dancer carries a peeled sumach stick. In the center of the dance circle is a bundle of fur or a stuffed beaver skin (formerly a dead beaver if possible); a bundle of rags with feathers attached has been used recently to represent "beaver." Occasionally a rope of Indian hemp fiber cordage is used instead of sticks to form the ring, and recently a store-bought rope was substituted for the fiber rope.

*First movement* (see fig. 10).—The men and women circle counter-clockwise with a shuffling step, holding a stick horizontally in the left hand. The end of each stick touches the next one, the touching ends being covered by the hand grasp. The sticks thus form a cordon or ring on the inside, supplemented by the dancers' hands. At a change of song they change sticks to the right hand, forming a ring or cordon of sticks outside the dancers.

*Second movement* (see fig. 11).—The dancers carry their sticks on the left shoulder like guns. A man and woman, representing hunters, dance inside the ring, repeatedly striking the stuffed beaver in the center of the circle. During this movement the man cries hyu, to which the dancers answer hyu. The beaver is attached to a string so that it may be jerked from outside the ring at the moment the dancers strike at it.

This is a pantomime of a beaver-hunting excursion by the hunter and his wife, the sticks representing beaver clubs (or guns). Four times during the dance the cry tɔyi′′ tɔyi′′, "beaver, beaver," is given,

# BEAVER DANCE
## FIRST MOVEMENT

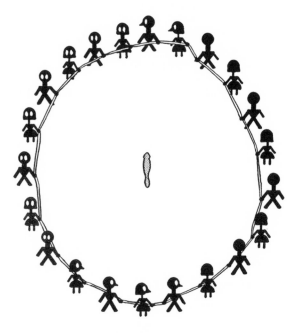

I : STICKS FORM CORDON ON INSIDE OF
      RING SUPPLEMENTED BY DANCERS' HANDS.
II : AT CHANGE OF SONG, CHANGE STICKS
      TO RIGHT HAND.
    : STUFFED BEAVER.

Figure 10

and the leader answers yo'hyo'. There is a divinatory notion in the hitting act. If the dancers repeatedly hit the beaver effigy it is a sign of good luck; if they miss it means bad luck. The dance lasts about half an hour.

# BEAVER DANCE
## SECOND MOVEMENT

MAN WHO JERKS BEAVER WHEN IT
IS HIT BY DANCERS.

Figure 11

**BUFFALO DANCE**

yan. 'sa, "buffalo"

*Equipment.*—There is a singer with a drum at one side of the group; the woman behind the leader wears turtle leg-rattles.

*Movement.*—A file of men followed by women circle counterclockwise with a continuous shuffling and stamping. There is mimicry of

( 71 )

buffalo by holding the fingers crooked upward at the temples to represent horns. The dancers utter hu' hu' in response to the leader's hano hε'.

This dance is reserved until toward morning in the series of night dances. A barbecue feast was formerly prepared to go with it. The features usually associated with the Buffalo Dance in other areas, such as the jostling of female dancers by male dancers—"cows" and "bulls," respectively—and the eating of corn mush from a bowl by the dancers, are lacking. Furthermore, the dance is not restricted to a society or to hunters; all are admitted.

It is interesting to note that the dance has persisted, even in this attenuated form, in spite of the disappearance of the buffalo from the Smokies perhaps a century and a half ago.

### PIGEON DANCE[26]

wɔyi'' ᴅākiɫanī', "pigeon going to roost," or ɑli: wɔt'adεkī:'', "jumping from one place to another"

*Equipment.*—A pile of hemlock twigs about 8 inches long, prepared by the leader, is at one side of the dance circle. The singer at the side of the circle has a gourd rattle and the two women behind the leader wear turtle leg-rattles.

*First movement.*—A close single file of men and women circle counterclockwise in a trot behind the leader.

*Second movement.*—Each dancer takes two hemlock twigs, waving them up and down like pigeons' wings.

*Third movement.*—A man, naked to the waist, his body painted red and his arms brown to represent a pigeon hawk,[27] rushes out from his hiding place at the side of the dance "yard" and charges the line of dancers, "pigeons," cutting it in two. The dancers separate, crying g', g', g', and shouting gã in alarm. The "pigeon hawk" may grab a dancer and carry him or her out of the dance line, as prey. (This event is timed to the utterance of syllables tcəni:hawɔ.)

*Fourth movement.*—The forward portion of the split dance ring continues onward; the rear portion turns and goes back until the two files meet and dance together as at the beginning.

*Fifth movement.*—The pigeon-hawk impersonator again cuts through the line of dancers, after which the dancers throw the hemlock twigs, "wings," on the ground.

In 1933 a Pigeon Dance was observed at Big Cove in which the pigeon-hawk actor carried an empty bag when he charged the dancers, slapping the bag on the ground among them. The "pigeons" did not use the hemlock twigs as wings. The "hawk" repeated his attack six times, circling around the dancers, threatening them before he rushed, and trying to capture any who were separated from the rest.

### PARTRIDGE DANCE

k‘kwɛ‛‛ (is whispered) aɫski:stï‘, "partridge dance." Because of the confusion of identity between birds and native bird names, this is often translated as the Quail Dance. (See Pl. XXI, *b*.)

*First movement.*—Two single files, men and women, each with its leader, circle in opposite directions to the accompaniment of a singer at one side, who has a drum. No rattles are used. In a performance of this dance at Bird Town in 1937, it was observed that the tempo retarded as the song level rose. When the leaders meet they advance side by side, the lines following the leaders.

*Second movement.*—Upon the signal yo‘hyo‘, the lines stop advancing and alternate, going forward and backward a few steps.

*Third movement.*—The lines separate and pass by each other, going in opposite directions again.

The imitative character of the dance is presumed to be based upon observation of the behavior of the birds by the ancients. West Long, in fantasy, projected himself into the tradition. He related that he had witnessed partridges dancing, like Indians, around a red oak on the

( 73 )

# Cherokee Dance and Drama

mountain; that they would whistle and bow down to each other occasionally, in the manner of the Friendship Dance.

oɢɑnã'ałski:stĩ'', "ground-hog dance"

*First movement.*—A double file, the men on the outside and the women on the inside as partners, circle counterclockwise to the accompaniment of a dance leader with gourd rattle and one or two women with leg-rattles. At the second strophe of the song the men change places with their partners.

*Second movement.*—The men dance backward, facing women partners for one strophe, then reverse with partners at the second.

The dancers motion toward their breasts, as though scooping up earth, to represent the burrowing and mound-heaping of the woodchuck.

səgwilĩ:'' ałski:stĩ'', "horse dance"

The mortar, which usually occupies the center of the room when dances are indoors, is taken out for this dance, since it requires a cleared square space for the movements.

*First movement.*—One or two straight rows of men abreast face northward toward the fire, near which is a singer with a drum. The dancers move forward in slow time with short steps, imitating the walk of a horse, and occasionally whinnying. At a whoop they about-face and retreat to the initial position, yelling ye' hye at each turn. This is repeated four times to four songs.

*Second movement.*—A woman wearing leg-rattles enters the row of dancers next to the man in the center of the row. The dancers, including the woman, hold hands and repeat the first movement in fast time, stomping hard with short steps, in imitation of the trotting and prancing of horses. They advance and return four times to four songs.

( 74 )

# Repertory of Dances

Formerly the men were said to have kicked at the women, in the manner of horses.

As in the Chicken Dance (below), the Horse Dance shows the admission of an acculturated property in Cherokee life on the same plane as native animal forces. One would expect to find this kind of acceptance by aboriginal forms, which were diversified to begin with, when the intrusive agent was essentially congruent. The horse and the chicken were introduced very early in contact history when the ceremonial forms were more elaborate than those catalogued here. On the other hand, we have no accounts of pig, dog, or cattle dances, and we may only conjecture whether these ever existed.

CHICKEN DANCE

tsəta:ga" ałski:stĩ", "chicken dance"

A single file of men and women, alternating partners, circle counterclockwise to the accompaniment of a singer at one side who uses either a drum or a gourd rattle. The dancers do not sing. At a change in the song the men dance backward, facing their women partners. Each dances on his left foot, raising the other off the ground, and the woman places her foot on the instep of her partner.

This is referred to as a friendship performance, illustrating the conduct of hen and cock, which is represented in the repetition in the song of the word wi:'a'skalelat'o, "chicken raises its leg."

According to West Long, only a few of the songs of this dance survived, and the singing lasts but ten to fifteen minutes. Its motivation is that of the friendship-inducing social dances taught by Stone Coat at the time of his death and ascent. The belief holds that Stone Coat revealed the coming of strange animals along with the new race (see the Booger Dance, p. 25)—the horse to ride upon, the "great hog" or plow, and the chicken or "the bird with something like red flint on head" (the comb). The dances, also revealed by Stone Coat, were to

( 75 )

incite friendly relations with the people who would come and the animals they would bring, as with the chicken. (See also the Horse Dance, p. 74.)

### KNEE-DEEP (SPRING FROG) DANCE

tu'stu'', onomatopoetic for voice of the diminutive tree frog, or spring
  peeper

*First movement.*—Two parallel lines of men and women circle counterclockwise in a slow, shuffling step. Each line has a singing leader, one of whom uses a gourd rattle after singing two songs; he is followed by a woman partner with turtle leg-rattles. At one side is a drummer, who does not sing, but all the dancers participate in the singing.

*Second movement.*—At change of song to quick time, all the dancers reverse direction.

*Third movement.*—The first movement is resumed.

The dance is popular for relaxation and sociability, and women are especially invited to participate.

### PISSANT DANCE

ɒəˈs.ã́' dattlĩ`, "small fly going up." "Pissant" is the old name by which
  the insect is known in the Carolinas. The term derives from the insect's habit of ejecting formic acid, supposedly for protection.

Two lines of dancers, representing trails of ants, circle in opposite directions in a shuffling trot. The leaders carry gourd rattles and each is followed by a woman wearing tortoise shell leg-rattles. The singing is done by the men. When the leaders meet they bow, retreat a few steps, then advance and pass on, leading their respective parties.

This dance, which lasts about ten minutes, belongs to the folk-dance category. It is popular because the song is simple and all the men engage in the singing. Its only function is social relaxation and friendship.

# Repertory of Dances

sɛlu′′, "corn." This is also the proper name of the the mistress of corn, known as Corn Woman.[28]

The male singer at one side of the circle has a gourd rattle but no drum. The men sing antiphonic responses to the leader. The woman behind the leader wears turtle leg-rattles.

*First movement.*—While advancing with a shuffling trot behind the leader, the men and women circle counterclockwise around the mortar in the center of the circle, making motions with their hands as though dipping and pouring corn or meal into a basket or bowl held in the other hand.

*Second movement.*—At a change in the song the women separate from the line, led by the woman with turtle leg-rattles. They circle the mortar and dance sideways, facing outward, surrounded by the men's line. The men face the women and, moving sideways, dance around the mortar for two or three turns. All continue the hand motions.

*Third movement.*—The men and women change places and, continuing the hand motions, make two or three circuits.

*Fourth movement.*—The lines of men and women mingle again and repeat the first movement.

In pouring corn from a bowl or "basket of plenty," the dancers express supplication and thanks for abundant corn crops. At one of these dances Will Pheasant took off his hat and, holding it in his left hand, motioned as though ladling corn into it with his other hand. He was one of the rare younger persons who participated in the dances in a creative way.

The Corn Dance is reserved for performance until toward morning in the night series, and is also a part of the night performances during the green corn ceremony (p. 45) in August. It follows the Friendship Dance (p. 65). It can be celebrated at any time, but it was formerly

( 77 )

# CORN DANCE

MORTAR

FIRST and FOURTH
MOVEMENTS

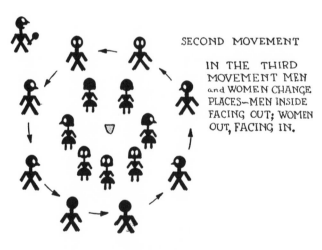

SECOND MOVEMENT

IN THE THIRD
MOVEMENT MEN
and WOMEN CHANGE
PLACES—MEN INSIDE
FACING OUT; WOMEN
OUT, FACING IN.

Figure 12

# Repertory of Dances

customary to rehearse it in early spring on the night before planting—the occasion t.tā'ni:wisī:ʾ, "they [community] are going to plant corn."

## RACCOON DANCE

kʻāʻlīʼʻałski:stīʻ, "raccoon dance"

A singer at the side of the group accompanies himself with a gourd rattle.

*First movement.*—A close single file of dancers has a leader, followed by a woman partner wearing tortoise shell leg-rattles. They circle counterclockwise in a shuffling trot.

*Second movement.*—The leader, while dancing backward facing his partner, goes through the motions of killing a raccoon with a club, skinning the carcass, stretching the skin on a frame, putting it away, scraping fat from the hide with a knife (or with the fingernails of both hands), and rubbing the grease on his partner's front and sides.

*Third movement.*—The first movement is repeated.

The Raccoon Dance has not been regularly performed since about 1890, and few besides West Long knew the song. There are no answers, singing, or yells by the dancers, but whether this is due to loss of these elements is not known.

## GIZZARD DANCE

Gãyuʻtʻan.aʼ, "gizzard lay down on the ground." Refers to the gizzard of any bird.

The musical accompaniment is provided by a gourd rattle and leg-rattles. Everyone whoops at the end of four repetitions of the song. The dancers are old men who, accompanied by a woman wearing leg-rattles, circle counterclockwise. They move with slow steps, stooping over and swaying their hind ends to swing "tails" of deerskin. The connections between the motions of the dancers and the purpose of the rite are not known.

( 79 )

# Cherokee Dance and Drama

This dance has been obsolete since about 1865. It was celebrated in the early fall, when the hunting of fowl began, and would continue with the turkey and partridge hunting through the winter. The rite was to prevent the people from becoming ill when they ate the gizzards of birds, which were considered a great delicacy. Malevolent conjurers were believed to use gizzards as a medium of infection; the dance, which provided immunity, was held every time wild fowl were killed.

### BAR-THE-WAY DANCE

ɢa"sɔhana:li", "across the rear side" (of something made of wood, as a bolt for a door)

The details and songs are not now known, for the dance probably has not been performed since the Cherokee Removal.

West Long's conception of the function of the dance was that it magically "barred the door of the house, or the gate of the settlement" against possible invasion in the dark by an enemy and prevented enemy conjurers from gaining admission in spirit disguise.

### WOMEN-GATHERING-WOOD DANCE

atɑho'nã", "make wood"

Only women participate, circling counterclockwise in a fashion indistinguishable from the usual Round Dance (p. 68) performance. They are accompanied by a male singer at one side, with a drum, who sings seven songs, in a gay mood. The women wear leg-rattles but do not sing.

The dance may express the functions of woman as a provider of wood for the dance fire, and woman's prestige as mistress of the hearth. Though rarely performed now, the dance was spontaneously included in dance cycles witnessed in 1935, 1936, and 1940. It may be given in any season. It comes early in the evening program, approximately before the Friendship Dance (p. 65).

# Repertory of Dances

This is the only Cherokee dance in which women may lead, though even in this the leader does not use the hand-rattle but wears leg-rattles. Besides its performance as a dance unit, it may have a more specific place in the Green Corn Dance and ceremony (p. 45).

## INTERMISSION PASTIMES

To keep the children occupied, the basket-dice game is brought out before the dances begin and in the intervals between dances. Adults also join in the game, which is a form of the widespread dice contest. It is called t'alu'ts.gā'dī'' a''kanios'ti:'yĭ, "with basket to play." Six dice, all alike and usually made of rhododendron wood, are carved in a variety of forms having no assigned symbolism except that some sets lanceolate in form are vaguely designated "fish." One side of the die is burned to make it dark. A shell basket, often the winnowing type, 8 to 12 inches across, is used. Among the Big Cove people, it is woven of oak splints in an under-two-over-two technique.[20] Small stakes may be wagered on the play, but the purpose is pastime and involves little skill and much chance.

The dice are thrown in and the basket thumped on lap, chair, or bed. There is no singing, but much hilarity. The counts are as follows: all dice white side up, 3; all black side up, 2; all but one same side up, 1. Other throws do not score. The game may be played for 12, 16, or 20 points, but usually for 12; and there may be two or more players or teams of players. The basket passes from left to right when the player fails to score in three throws. Local forms of the same game, using a wooden bowl instead of the basket, are played under the same circumstances among Eastern tribes as far west as the Osage.

## CONTESTS AT CONCLUSION OF DANCE NIGHT

At the conclusion of the night dances the Cherokee gathering in the Big Cove settlement does not hurriedly disperse, even though the

# Cherokee Dance and Drama

dancing may have continued until eight or nine o'clock in the gloomy log house shrouded in morning mists and shut off from the sun by battened windows. We have observed that the dancers are frequently unaware of the dawn until the sun lights the upper heights of the sheltering mountains, when the Driver calls for the final Round or Running Dance (p. 68).

Then, quitting the dwelling, the celebrants assemble in the yard for a last social festivity. At this time one of the games or contests is held between the men and the women to decide who shall, within the week, give a feast to the community. Since the Big Cove people used to dance on Saturday nights, the feast was usually appointed for the following Friday night. West Long said that the custom had been abandoned since the turn of the century.

The ensuing descriptions cover the details of two game contests, the Tug of War and the Football Game, in which men and women form opposing sides. If the men lose, the feast will be of meat and the men will go on the hunt; if the women lose, the food will be corn bread or meal. These feasts were free to all who came. The game contests were not accompanied by singing, nor do we learn of symbolism or spiritual associations in their movements.[30] It is clear, however, that the basic division of labor is represented in the two menus.

In the Tug of War (di:da:se'sã'.di':yi:', "pulling against each other," or dãnasɛ'sãhĩ'), sides were chosen to include ten or more men on one side, with a strong woman to take first place, and an equal number of women on the other side, with a strong man to head them. The sides pulled on a grapevine in an attempt to pull their opponents over a line drawn on the ground. Each side had a male driver to spur them on.

The Football Game (alaskã'ł.di:yi:', "putting the ball in [the goal]") functioned in the same manner. A hard, heavy ball of deerskin, about 3 inches in diameter, was made and goals were set up. As many as wished to play were arranged on opposite sides, the women led by a man and the men by a woman. They rushed at the ball to kick it through the opposite goal; the game ended at the first score. There is no mention of conjuring the ball, the goals, or the players in the tradition of this game, which has not been seen since the turn of the century.

# 3.

# Animal Hunting Formulas and Rites

THIS section concerns the chanted formulas used in connection with hunting and the methods of approaching and securing game. According to Cherokee teachings, the songs for dancing and the formulas for hunting are of one genus, derived from the events narrated in the Stone Coat origin tale (pp. 13–18). In using the hunting formulas for specified animals, the hunter must restrict himself to killing the animal for which he has prayed. Thus, when going for bear, other game must not be killed until a bear has been taken. To violate this regulation would spoil the hunter's luck.

An important doctrine of the hunting-formula procedure is that animals called out and killed by hunters who employ the formulistic magic come back to life again. Thus there is no diminution in the supply of game animals through hunting.

In this connection Mooney and Olbrechts comment:

a variety of conjurations and songs . . . aim at bringing success in hunting and fishing. Some of the hunting formulas are also used in divination practices, which are reputed to advise the hunter as to whether the time he has chosen to go on a hunting expedition is propitious, in which direction he has to depart, what he will kill and when.

There is no doubt but that almost all the men knew a couple or more of

# Formulas and Rites

these specimens some generations ago, when hunting, and even big-game hunting, were events of almost daily occurrence.

The hunters bought the knowledge of these songs and formulas from the medicine men, as much as $5 being paid for a bear-hunting song some 50 years ago. Now, as hunting is reduced to shooting rabbits and other small game, and with the advent of shotguns, there no longer seems to be so much call for this magic ammunition, and the formulas have therefore reverted to the custody of the medicine men.

Dr. Olbrechts did not include any specimens of this series in the manuscripts published in the joint collection.[1]

## LARGE ANIMAL HUNTING MASKS

Traditionally, wooden decoy masks were used by the Cherokee in hunting the buffalo, bear, and deer. The hunter who went on an individual excursion used the appropriate mask. As a means of ceremonial approach to the animal he would, before departing, wear the mask in a dance; and on the hunt would carry the mask and the skin of the animal. As soon as he located his game he would place the mask over his face and the skin over his back to serve as a disguise, it is said, to enable him to approach the animal without arousing suspicion. He would keep himself, of course, on a line against the wind so that the animal would not become alarmed by human scent. Then, the informant says, "The hunter would shoot the animal, *using the magic* of the mask." Upon returning from the hunt, should it have proved successful, the hunter might repeat the Hunting Dance, using the mask in the same manner as he did before his hunt. We are told that if the hunt were a drive, carried on by a party of men, the mask might be worn by only one of them. When the hunt was over and many animals had been killed, the hunting party would give a special dance about a fire and celebrate with a feast.

Specimens of decoy masks are shown in Plates VIII and IX. On the foreheads are tacked bosses of fur, indiscriminately bear, rabbit,

---

[1] For notes to chapter 3 see page 102.

woodchuck, opossum, muskrat, and gray fox, but the bear masks have a patch of the appropriate skin. The relative strength of the bear symbol may be inferred from this fact. We may conjecture that when the various animals were abundant in the Smokies, the "correct" skins would generally have been used. The bear masks are stained black with walnut-bark dye and the eyeholes often painted red. The buffalo mask is similar to the bear mask in form and dark color, with, however, conspicuous incurved horns on the forehead and a boss of fur of some kind. (See Pl. IX.) The buffalo and deer masks are stained dark red with sumach stain and red clay; the eyeholes are edged with black. The wildcat mask shown (see Pl. VIII) is of leather with wildcat and horsehair trimmings. It was used in hunting the wild turkey.

At this late date the use of the buffalo mask can only be inferred. Buffalo hunters probably used them in the dance held before and after the hunt, as well as for decoy purposes. According to West Long, the buffalo mask was a parallel of the deer mask, but no one could be found who remembered the appropriate buffalo-mask formulas. West Long's comment was as follows: "Those masks were used when they went out buffalo hunting together, with skins on their bodies, as they represented live buffalo so they could come close to them."

### Bear Hunting Formulas

We have already commented on the preëminence of the bear in Cherokee belief, but a legend recorded by Mooney may be repeated: "The bears were the first to meet in council in their townhouse in Kuwahi, the 'Mulberry Place' [one of the high peaks of the Smoky Mountains, on the Tennessee line, near Clingman's Dome], and the old White Bear chief presided. After each in turn had made complaint against the way in which man killed their friends, devoured their flesh and used their skins for his own self-adornment, it was unanimously decided to begin war against the human race." Then follows a narration of the means considered for defense, the explanation of

# Formulas and Rites

bear and human antagonism, and the final indignity that the hunter does not even ask the bear's pardon when he kills him.[2] The place Kuwahi referred to is the same location as in the bear hunting song formula given below.

In reference to the origin of the bear songs, Mooney recorded a tale of a nonextant clan, the Ani'-Tsâgûhi, who voluntarily abandoned the life and form of human beings and became a company of bears. To accomplish the transformation, these people abstained from food for seven days and had the will to live in the woods as a "drove of bears." Said they, as they departed, "We are going where there is always plenty to eat. Hereafter we shall be called *yanu* (bears), and when you yourselves are hungry come into the woods and call us and we shall come to give you our own flesh. You need not be afraid to kill us, for we shall live always." To the tale is appended an account of the origin of the songs, which is a variant of the legend of the Stone Coat. Supernaturalism among the forest people has its inconsistencies too. "Then they taught the messengers the songs with which to call them, and the bear hunters have these songs still."[3]

Mooney, fortunately, preserved two specimens of bear hunting song formulas, which are given in abbreviated form.

FIRST BEAR SONG

He-e! Ani'-Tsâgûhi, Ani'-Tsâgûhi,

akwandu'li e'lanti' ginûn'ti

He-e! The Ani'-Tsâgûhi, the Ani'-Tsâgûhi,

I want to lay them low on the ground.

(Sung twice with Yû! at the finish.)

The bear hunter starts out in the morning fasting and does not eat until near evening. He sings this song as he leaves each camp and again the next morning, but never twice the same day.

( 87 )

# Cherokee Dance and Drama

This song is also sung by the bear hunter, in order to attract the bears, while on his way from the camp to the place where he expects to hunt during the day. The melody is simple and plaintive.

> He-e! Hayuya′ haniwă′, hayuya′ haniwă′, hayuya′ haniwă′, hayuya′ haniwă′,
> Tsistúyi′ nehandu′ yanû′, Tsistúyi′ nehandu′ yanû—Yoho-o!

The same lines are sung four times. At each repetition the first word of the second line is changed from Tsistúyi′ to the following, which are names of gorges where bears dwell: Kuwâ′hi, Uyâ′hye, Gâte′gwâ.

> (Recited) Ulĕ-'nû′ asĕhĭ′ tadeyâ′ statakûhĭ′ gûñ′năge astû′ tsĭkĭ.
> He-e! Hayuyá haniwă′ (four times). In Tsistu′yĭ you were conceived (two times). Yoho-o!

In the three ensuing verses the places Kuwâ′hĭ, Uyâ′hye, Gâte′gwâ are substituted for Tsistu′yi′.

> (Recited) And now surely we and the good black things, the best of all, shall see each other.

Corresponding to the foregoing formula, recorded by Mooney half a century ago, is a version taken down in 1935 from Wesley Driver, aged sixty-seven, who was taught the formula by his father. It is a prayer calling for bears to come out of their inaccessible places. In the transcription by Dr. Herzog, we note that the text follows rather closely that given by Mooney, repeating certain of the place names in his text and adding others.

kuwɔ′hi, "mulberries, where there are"

This refers to Kuwohi, a deep, dark ravine at the head of Deep Creek near the Tennessee–North Carolina state line.

# Formulas and Rites

a'dagohĭ, "gall, where it is"

Refers to a location near Clingman's Dome where there is supposed to be a lake of yellowish water looking like gall, but nevertheless good to drink. It is hidden to all ordinary hunters, who see only a swamp; but to the hunter who knows the song and who faithfully observes the rules of fasting for a day and a night, staying awake all night, will be granted the boon of finding the lake of "gall," a place of danger but abounding in wild fowl.

sa′n.ə galɔ, "something sticking out like a rocky promontory"

Refers to a place near Culhowee, North Carolina, a wild, rocky ravine where the Cherokee believed the Thunders to live.

u:yɔ′hĭ, "no good, dangerous, place"

Refers to a noted resort of bears at the head of the center fork of Oconaluftee Creek, on the side where Bradley's Creek is located.

The following bear hunting formula was acquired long ago by West Long. It was sung before and after the hunt and with or without the bear mask.

ɢa'kwɛ'nṹ:, "all done up [in a buckskin bundle]" (meaning that the bear's meat is ready to carry away—the hunt successful)
di:ha′', "is there now"
ya'ya' (imitating bear)
sa lu'ye kwɔ, "roughest extensive place" (place favored by bears)
ta du'yɑna, "that's where you originated" (as though asking the bear to start this way)
wa tak' ta' (spoken) "he has a white spot on the neck"

## DEER HUNTING FORMULAS

To bring the deer within the power of the hunter and his weapons, certain songs were rehearsed preparatory to departure for the hunt, and we shall refer again to Mooney's observations on the nature and origin of deer hunting formulas. The legend given below is from that part of the myth of Kana'ti and Selu which relates to the final acts of the son of this pair of mythical parents and his companion, Wild Boy, who originated from the blood of game slain by Kana'ti. Kana'ti was the mythical owner of the game animals, which he kept in a cave in the mountains. Selu, his wife, was the patron deity of corn, which is denoted by the same term. The boys, known as "Kana'ti's boys," seem to personify thunder and lightning. The deer hunting songs refer to the boys' discovery of the cave where the deer and other animals were kept by Kana'ti, and the release of the animals to roam the woods where they are chased and killed. The account is as follows:

After Kana'ti's boys had let the deer out from the cave where their father used to keep them, the hunters tramped about in the woods for a long time without finding any game, so that the people were very hungry. At last they heard that the Thunder Boys were now living in the far west, beyond the sun door, and that if they were sent for they could bring back the game. So they sent messengers for them, and the boys came and sat down in the middle of the townhouse and began to sing.

At the first song there was a roaring sound like a strong wind in the northwest, and it grew louder and nearer as the boys sang on, until at the seventh song a whole herd of deer, led by a large buck, came out from the woods. The boys had told the people to be ready with their bows and arrows, and when the song was ended and all the deer were close around the townhouse, the hunters shot into them and killed as many as they needed before the herd could get back into the timber.

Then the Thunder Boys went back to the Darkening Land, but before they left they taught the people the seven songs with which to call up the deer. It all happened so long ago that the songs are now forgotten—all but two, which the hunters still sing whenever they go after deer.[4]

It is not our purpose to draw analogies between Cherokee beliefs and their legendary origins and those of other tribes of the Southeast. We are tempted, however, to refer to Swanton's mention of the Biloxi tale of the animals kept in houses by One-Above, who showed them to Indians coming to see him. Buffaloes, bears, deer, lightning giant,

# Formulas and Rites

and garments were there. The animals were to remain in the house, "but a boy was so bad that he opened a door and let them out, therefore they are in the swamps (*sic:* probably on the prairies)."[5]

Mooney's material, obtained before 1900, comes from an important period of the tribe's history and is a valuable check on later sources. Although we note discrepancies between his accounts of the origin of the hunting song formulas and the tale dictated by West Long, there is no point in seeking a rigid consistency. Whether the hunting songs alternatively originate in the blessed sacrifice of the deadly monster Stone Coat or from the teachings of the mischievous Thunder Boys need not be regarded as a defect in native powers of reasoning. There is nothing necessarily "wrong" with the coexistence of alternative explanations, and variant versions of origins occur in other ancient tribal literatures than Genesis.

The tale just outlined credits the Cherokee with knowing only two of the deer hunting songs, which it seems Mooney did not take down, but here at least is one of the series from West Long.

| he ɢa' a nu: si: ni: | his head is nearly always near the ground |
| si: yu' tsi ła yu' sti:' | he smells something unpleasant [human beings] in his nose |
| he tsa ha no li: dɔ̃ha' | he has a stalking [stealthy] nature |
| onɑ̃ ta' si ha si: han | he was alone at the top of the ledge |

The hunter would rehearse the song before and after the deer hunt and, anciently, the deer mask would be worn. Should sufficient game be killed, the singer would wear the mask and lead a dance with his companions and guests at a feast of the meat.

Besides the use of the deer decoy and representative mask, the Cherokee, like other peoples of the Southeast and the Central Algonkian area, employed a deer call when stalking, to imitate and lure the fawn or doe according to circumstance and season. Specimens of the instrument made by Kaloski Standing Deer were 4 inches long, of split laurel twig, with a piece of laurel or rhododendron leaf length-wise in the cleft as a vibrator. When the operator sucks, the air strikes the vibrator, producing a musical buzzing. It is similar in principle to ribbon reed.

## TURKEY HUNTING FORMULAS

The means bequeathed to the Cherokee by the Stone Coat for the hunting and capture of the wild turkey included hunting song formulas exerting magic power over the bird to call it forth from its cover, knowledge of means to decoy it within range of the hunter's weapon, and power to imitate its calls. The decoy call is a simple tube made from the wing or leg bone of the bird, which, inserted in the corner of the mouth, can be made by suction to emit a chirping call.

It is usual for the hunter to hide himself under a thick mat of green moss (*Hypnum curvifolium* Hedwig), which abounds in the heights where the turkeys hide during the day. A strip of the moss, 3 by 5 feet, is used as a covering. In the strip of moss, the hunter cuts eyeholes, above which he inserts two upright leaves (chestnut, laurel, or rhododendron) to simulate the ears of the wildcat. The disguise apparently serves two purposes: to enable the hunter to approach the game, and by imitative magic to gain some of the skills of stealth of the cat. In addition to the moss disguise, the hunter might wear a mask of untanned, stiff skin (often woodchuck), provided with ear tufts formed by projections of the skin or by deer tails. The nose is a separate piece of the woodchuck skin.

### TURKEY HUNTING SONGS

The following song formula for wild turkey hunting was owned by Wesley Driver, who had bought it in his youth from a medicine man.

it'ɛ'       we are living [in one cove]
ta' suyɔ'   [we are] scratching, spreading leaves (repeated four times)
tɑk tɑk     (imitation of turkey's voice)
tɑk' lu'    (imitation of turkey's gobble)

# Formulas and Rites

In another song from Wesley Driver the words are softly intoned and rather low.

su'sa hi: lə gi:     at a flat, level cove
hi: tsi to su yo' ga'    you scratching there [your legs sinking in the earth]
su'kɛ' t'a li:yū'    in just one cove [scratching]
su la ga     (no meaning)

West Long did not possess turkey hunting songs, although his step-brother had used them successfully. Besides using the song formulas, hunting rules, and the skin mask, he painted black lines from nose to ears with charcoal and grease. Fastening green leaves in his hair, he would lie beside a log, awaiting the chance to shoot. One song is as follows:

su'kɛ' t'a li:yū'    in just one cove [scratching]
hi: tsi: ɒə'su hɛ̃'    scratching about under leaves [tail feathers spread first on one side, then on the other]
hi: tsi:ɒə' su yɔ 'ɢa'   scratching about now in the cove

## Eagle Hunting Formula

Hunting the eagle is a very particular act. To call the eagle from the air the hunter uses a song, which is also part of the Eagle Dance. West Long learned it from his brother years ago when they saw an eagle soaring above them and succeeded in calling it within reach. By this song West Long on several subsequent occasions called eagles from the upper heights nearly to the ground.

The Eagle-Killer must go on the hunt without eating anything. He calls the eagle within range, then shoots it.° While it lies on the ground the killer sings the song again, but before the feathers are pulled out the body must be treated ceremonially lest a kind of "maggot" infest the killer and cause his death. Feathers are to the Cherokee spiritual agencies of considerable power. For example, they believe that to wear buzzard or turkey feathers on the head or to use them in

# Cherokee Dance and Drama

filling pillows will cause baldness. Leaving the eagle on the ground, without touching it, the hunter cuts seven hand-length sticks of sourwood (*Oxydendrum arboreum* Linn.), sharpens one end, and plants them like a fence around the bird. Then he goes home and fetches four men who have fasted in preparation for pulling the feathers. This done, they leave the body to avoid contamination. The feathers, which are ready to be used for Eagle Dance wands, are put away where no one else will touch them. The party may then eat. The Eagle-Killer receives a reward of gifts ("sacrifices") during an interval of the Booger Dance (p. 25).

### Hunting Song Formula for General Use

Besides the specific forms of ritual preparation for approaching and attacking game, there is at least one generalized hunting song. It is, like the rest, a personal possession to be shared with others only upon the receipt of payment or, from the native point of view, "sacrifice." West Long, who recalled obtaining the song from his father, used it before going on any hunting excursion to "bring success in hunting in general." He repeated it at night before lying down to sleep and also in the morning before starting out. Continence and fasting were prescribed until something was killed. The phrases are:

| | |
|---|---|
| ka′na:tiʻ | successful hunter (Kana′ti, the hero of the game-release myth and the mythical patron of hunters)[7] |
| henadṏ′sihɛ̃ | come together and act in unison |
| sɔgwoʻhĭ | two become together one |
| henadṏ′sihɛ̃ | come together and act in unison |
| sónɔĭ: | night |
| henadṏ′sihɛ̃ | come together and act in unison |
| ka′na:tiʻ | successful hunter |
| henadṏ′sihɛ̃ | come together and act in unison |
| ya ya ya ya | (no meaning) |

( 94 )

# Formulas and Rites

Olbrechts noted that this hunting formula would have commanded a high price, at least five dollars, some years ago when hunting was good; but now its owner does not consider it worth holding as a personal, secret property. As in all the dances and formulas, the opportunity is rapidly passing to rescue the lore from oblivion. Here a peculiar crisis is produced by the loss in value of a property which makes it more accessible to the research worker at the same time that its cultural retention becomes less likely.

The hunting songs and many of the Cherokee medicinal songs contain an implicit attitude toward the animal world which is also suggested in the dances and folk tales. Animals are considered fundamentally antagonistic toward humans, and are especially to be feared when they must be exploited as an economic resource or otherwise injured through human activities. Hunting songs and other ritualistic forms of the hunter and trapper are supernaturalistic methods of making animals subject to humans, and of minimizing the retaliation of the spirits of the slain animal and his kinsmen. These spirit agents, called sʻkɛʹ.nɑʻ, a human or animal ghost, are still regarded as dreaded agents of disease by the conservative Cherokee. The term sʻkɛʹ.nɑʻ is the name for the Devil in Cherokee Biblical translations, and is colloquial usage among the more acculturated Cherokee speakers. Animals differ in their power, but the ghosts even of the insignificant ants may wreak havoc by spirit intrusion. Some formulas and ritual procedures are prophylactic against retaliation by injured animal forms, and many of the medicinal formulas are specific curative processes intended to control and exorcise animal spirits held responsible for disease, just as the hunting formula makes the living animal subject to the speaker.

Community rituals and dances are also in large part devoted to animal dances and pantomime, and may placate and exorcise the animal spirit world. In each of these aspects Cherokee culture resembles the Creek, whose animal dances make up a large part of recurrent community ritual. The Creek also have in the Busk a gun dance much like Cherokee. Their hunting and medicinal formulas deal with animals and spirits in a similar fashion, and a similar attitude toward zoölogical supernaturalism prevails. The Creek and Cherokee differ from Iroquois, Delaware, and other more northerly peoples, who see the animal world in a state of friendly symbiosis with the human community. Even in everyday life, the Seminole and Cherokee show a brutality toward animals unusual among the northern peoples. This is explicit in the Beaver Dance. Among the Cherokee ritual and formula grant immunity or protection from the spirit agents of the animal world with which man wages an unequal war.

# NOTES

# NOTES

## Notes to Chapter 1

[1] Sachs, 1947, p. 4.

[2] Mooney and Olbrechts, 1932.

[3] Refer to Cherokee theories of the maintenance and protection of life, as discussed by Mooney (1891, pp. 318–324) and Olbrechts (Mooney and Olbrechts, 1932, pp. 17–29; especially pp. 25–26, animal spirits) for an understanding of the underlying principles of human adjustment to the realms of animals, plants, and men.

[4] Schwarze, 1923, p. 212.

[5] *Ibid.*, p. 203.

[6] The material cited from the Payne MS in Squier's notes to Bartram, 1853, p. 74, is erroneous in several instances. Squier, without noting his change, wrote "tribe" where Payne correctly had "clan." Squier also misread or miscorrected a number of Payne's renderings of Cherokee words. We take the opportunity here to set the record straight. Payne MS I, ll. 70–71, from the Ayer Collection, by courtesy of the Newberry Library.

[7] This initiated the gogi summer months.

[8] This is the festival in fragmentary form which seems to have survived all the others.

[9] This signaled the beginning of the gola winter months.

[10] During this celebration, reconciliation was the keynote and even revenge obligations might be abrogated. Such a motif occurs in other ceremonies, and plays a very important part in the Boos-ke-tau, during which a general amnesty was provided. The aborigines were absolved from all crimes with the occasional exception of murder, and the guilt itself seems to have been expunged through some social participation of the community. It is likely that loss of such solidarities and social functions as this, difficult to isolate and evaluate, were the most significant and far-reaching events of the early period. The Ah,tawh,hung,nah festival is probably to be identified with the Busk, general in the Southeast. (See Hawkins' description of the Boos-ke-tau in Bartram, 1853, pp. 67 ff.)

[11] Tuttle, 1833, pp. 147–153. This item was supplied through the courtesy of John Witthoft. The principal source is Charles Hicks, referred to below, chapter 2, note 14.

[12] Mooney and Olbrechts, 1932, pp. 150, 232–233.

[13] In the Big Cove this tale is given as the origin story for the marble game, in Bird Town as the origin story for the Chunky Game. Witthoft, ND.

[14] Mooney, 1900, pp. 319–320. Mooney also published a short version of the same myth. Mooney, 1888, p. 98.

[15] Mooney and Olbrechts, 1932, p. 146.

# Cherokee Dance and Drama

## NOTES TO CHAPTER 2

[1] Personal information.

[2] Mooney and Olbrechts, 1932, facing p. 117.

[3] *Ibid.*, p. 121.

[4] As John Witthoft points out, in his paper (1949) on Cherokee pipes, some of the ideas of the calumet rite as introduced into the Southeast and described in several early sources seem to have survived to the present as a major feature in several Cherokee rituals. The Eagle Dance seems to be itself a transparent survival of part of the older calumet rite. The whole pattern of the Booger Dance shows calumet motifs. The impersonation of strange people and of their dangerous spiritual counterparts is an example of the projection of Cherokee attitudes and emotions toward Europeans, who have been the instrument of their cultural disintegration. Relief is found in making concrete, and therefore tangible and manageable, the terrifying sense of oppression by aliens. This drama is not the whole of the pattern, however. The appearance and introduction of the Boogers is followed by two variants of the calumet rite. That the Boogers may call for the Eagle Dance is an indication that the Boogers might ask to be placed on a plane of friendship and coöperation with the Cherokee in a binding ritual form. The smoking rite for the singers and the rite of rewarding the Eagle-Killer in this sequence seem to indicate the essential calumet ritual nature of the sequence; it is a single modern phase of the calumet ceremony in which an actual calumet is smoked and passed around. Most of the surviving Cherokee specimens used in this rite are bear-effigy pipes, indicating some close but poorly understood linkage between the calumet rite variants and the Bear Dance, which alternates with the Eagle Dance in the Booger Dance sequence. Other calumet motifs and functional parallels to the calumet rite may be seen in the War or Snake-Mask Dance and the Scalp Dance, especially in the greeting of dancers with feather wands and scalps as a primary aspect of the Scalp Dance.

[5] For an account of the restrictions, including prayer and fasting, which are placed upon the Eagle-Killer by the Cherokee, see Mooney, 1900, pp. 281–283. He refers to the offerings made at the dance and gives in detail the method by which the eagle is ceremonially killed and its remains disposed of. The killing is blamed upon a Spaniard. Eagles could be killed only after crops were gathered and snakes had retired to their dens, an instance of the legendary enmity between eagles and serpents which is widespread in America.

[6] Mooney and Olbrechts, 1932, p. 132.

[7] *Ibid.*, p. 41.

[8] Dr. John R. Swanton identified this location and pointed out a chart of the section in J. W. Barnwell, "The Second Tuscarora Expedition," *South Carolina Historical and Genealogical Magazine* (Charleston, S.C.), Vol. X (1909), map, p. 33.

[9] Lawson, 1714 (edition of 1860), p. 68.

[10] For an account of the ritual undertaken by the Eagle-Killer who secures eagle feathers (golden eagle, according to Mooney) for the wands, and a sketch of a

# Notes

wand, see Mooney, 1900, pp. 281–283 and fig. 1. Also, see Booger Dance (p. 33), interlude, for ritual payment of the Eagle-Killer.

[11] Mooney, 1900, p. 283.

[12] *Ibid.*, p. 281.

[13] Timberlake, 1765, pp. 36–39.

[14] "Manners, Customs, &c." of the Cherokee Indians, by Charles Hicks, second chief of the nation in 1818, who had been converted by the Moravians in 1812. The manuscript was written by Hicks at the request of Mr. Hoyt, a missionary, and was copied by Calvin Jones. Jones sent it in a letter dated October 13, 1818, to Mr. Gales, apparently editor of the *Raleigh Register,* in which journal it was printed. The excerpt from which this was taken is in the Bureau of American Ethnology *Scrapbook*, Vol. I, l. 354, compiled by J. R. Swanton.

[15] Mooney (1900, p. 492) stated that these men purified themselves by "going to the water" beforehand.

[16] In 1935 Going Bird was the accepted voluntary officiator in the song leadership of the women's part. Sherman and John Taylor sang it for recording in 1936.

[17] Bureau of American Ethnology *Scrapbook,* Vol. I, l. 354, compiled by J. R. Swanton.

[18] One of the minor differences in the rites as performed in different Cherokee towns is brought out in the observation by West Long that when the Green Corn Dance is celebrated by the Bird Town settlement the men in this movement carry their guns aloft, grasped in both hands by stock and barrel, alternately leaning forward, placing the guns on the ground, and raising them, as one remarked, in "Pueblo style."

[19] Mooney, 1900, p. 396.

[20] Witthoft, 1946.

[21] Schwarze, 1923, pp. 78–79.

[22] The pregame and new-fire rituals are discussed in Witthoft's manuscript, "Eastern Cherokee Games."

[23] This bird derives its Cherokee name from its call, tal-u-la-r-r-r. The name has also become a family patronym in the Eastern band.

[24] Mooney and Olbrechts, 1932, pp. 68–70.

[25] Hodge, 1910, p. 636–637.

[26] Witthoft and Fenton have collected a roc story believed to be the origin myth for the Pigeon Dance.

[27] Probably the broad-winged hawk (*Buteo platypterus*). Cf. Mooney, 1900, p. 284, who thought it was the goshawk (*Astur atricapillus*).

[28] See p. 90, Hunting Song Formulas; also Witthoft, 1946.

[29] Speck, 1920, Plate XV, figs. 1, 4, 6, 7.

[30] The student of eastern Indian rituals will note that the Iroquois perform both these "games" as medicine rites in the series of ceremonials connected with the annual celebrations of the Long House (Speck, 1949, pp. 124–126). The same observation applies to the bear sacrifice ceremony of the Canadian Delawares.

# Cherokee Dance and Drama

## NOTES TO CHAPTER 3

[1] Mooney and Olbrechts, 1932, p. 153.

[2] Mooney, 1891, pp. 319–320.

[3] Mooney and Olbrechts, 1932, pp. 325–326, and 326–327 for the song texts.

[4] Mooney, 1900, p. 248. Witthoft (1946) secured some interesting additional details of this origin myth.

[5] Swanton, 1912, p. 54.

[6] Eagle hunting, without mention of the trap method, is described by Mooney, 1900, pp. 281–282.

[7] *Ibid.*, p. 248; also p. 90 of this study.

# BIBLIOGRAPHY

# BIBLIOGRAPHY

BENDER, ERNEST, AND ZELLIG S. HARRIS
    1946    The Phonemes of North Carolina Cherokee. *International Journal of American Linguistics*, Vol. 12, No. 1, pp. 14-21.

BUTTERFIELD, L. H., WILCOMB E. WASHBURN, AND WILLIAM N. FENTON
    1957    *American Indian and White Relations to 1830: A Bibliography.* In Fenton, 1957.

FENTON, WILLIAM N.
    1957    *American Indian and White Relations to 1830: Needs and Opportunities for Study.* The University of North Carolina Press, Chapel Hill.

GILBERT, WILLIAM H., JR.
    1943    The Eastern Cherokees. Anthropological Papers no. 23, Smithsonian Institution, Bureau of American Ethnology, *Bulletin* 133, pp. 169-413. Washington, D.C.

HALLOWELL, A. IRVING
    1951    Frank Gouldsmith Speck, 1881-1950. *American Anthropologist,* Vol. 53, No. 1, pp. 67-75.

HODGE, FREDERICK WEBB (ed.).
    1910    Handbook of American Indians North of Mexico. Smithsonian Institution, Bureau of American Ethnology, *Bulletin* 30. Washington, D.C.

KILPATRICK, ANNA GRITTS, AND JACK FREDERICK KILPATRICK
    1966    Chronicles of Wolftown: Social Documents of the North Carolina Cherokee, 1850-1862. Anthropological Papers No. 75, Smithsonian Institution, Bureau of American Ethnology, *Bulletin* 196, pp. 1-111. Washington, D.C.

LAWSON, JOHN
    1714    *History of North Carolina.* London, 1714; Raleigh, 1860; Charlotte, 1903.

MOONEY, JAMES
    1888    Myths of the Cherokees. *Journal of American Folklore,* Vol. 1, pp. 97-108.
    1890a   The Cherokee Ball Play. *American Anthropologist,* Vol. 3, pp. 105-132.

# Bibliography

1890*b* Cherokee Theory and Practice of Medicine. *Journal of American Folklore,* Vol. 3, pp. 44-50.

1891 The Sacred Formulas of the Cherokee. Smithsonian Institution, Bureau of American Ethnology, *Seventh Annual Report.* Washington, D.C.

1900 Myths of the Cherokee. Smithsonian Institution, Bureau of American Ethnology, *Nineteenth Annual Report,* Part 1. Washington, D.C.

MOONEY, JAMES, AND FRANS M. OLBRECHTS
1932 The Swimmer Manuscript, Cherokee Sacred Formulas and Medical Prescriptions. Smithsonian Institution, Bureau of American Ethnology, *Bulletin* 99.Washington, D.C.

OLBRECHTS, FRANS M.
1929 Prophylaxis in Cherokee Medicine. *Janus,* Archives Internationales pour l'Histoire de la Médecine et la Géographie Médicale, 33^me année, pp. 18-22. Leyden.

PAYNE, JOHN HOWARD
The Ayers Collection of Americana. Newberry Library of University of Chicago. 14 vols. MS.

SACHS, WULF
1947 *Black Hamlet.* Boston, Mass.

SCHWARZE, EDMUND
1923 *History of the Moravian Missions among Southern Indian Tribes of the United States.* Transactions of the Moravian Historical Society, Special Series, Vol. 1. Bethlehem, Pa.

SPECK, FRANK G.
1920 *Decorative Art and Basketry of the Cherokees.* Bulletin of the Museum of the City of Milwaukee, Vol. 2, No. 2.

1949 *Midwinter Rites of the Cayuga Long House.* University of Pennsylvania Press, Philadelphia.

SWANTON, JOHN R., AND JAMES OWEN DORSEY
1912 A Dictionary of the Biloxi and Ofo Languages. Smithsonian Institution, Bureau of American Ethnology, *Bulletin* 47. Washington, D.C.

TIMBERLAKE, LIEUTENANT HENRY
1927 *Memoirs, 1756-1765.* S. C. Williams (ed.). Johnson City, Tenn.

# Bibliography

TUTTLE, SARAH
  1833   *Letters and Conversations on the Cherokee Mission.* 2d ed., Massa-
         chusetts Sabbath School Society, Boston.

WALKER, WILLARD
  1965   *Cherokee Primer.* Carnegie Corporation Cross-Cultural Education
         Project of the University of Chicago. Tahlequah, Oklahoma.

WITTHOFT, JOHN
  1946   The Cherokee Green Corn Medicine and the Green Corn Festival.
         *Journal of the Washington Academy of Sciences,* Vol. 36, No. 7,
         pp. 213-219.
  ND     Eastern Cherokee Games. Unpublished MS.
  1948   Will West Long, Cherokee Informant. *American Anthropologist,*
         Vol. 50, No. 2, pp. 355-359.
  1949   Stone Pipes of the Historic Cherokees. *Southern Indian Studies,*
         Vol. 1, No. 2, pp. 43-62.
  1951   Anthropological Bibliography of Frank G. Speck, 1903-1950. *Amer-
         ican Anthropologist,* Vol. 53, No. 1, pp. 75-87.

# INDEX

# Cherokee Dance and Drama

# Index

# Cherokee Dance and Drama